YOUR FRIENDSHIP WITH HOLY SPIRIT

OTHER BOOKS BY SARAH BOWLING

Hey God, Can We Talk?

*How to Keep Your Faith
in an Upside Down World*

*In Step with the Spirit—Infusing Your Life
With God's Presence and Power*

*Heavenly Help—Experiencing the
Holy Spirit in Everyday Life*

Jesus Chicks

Jesus is God's Selfie

Save Your Fork—There's More!

30 Meditations on Healing (with Marilyn Hickey)

30 Meditations on the Names of God (with Marilyn Hickey)

Hanging by a Thread—The Saving Moses Journey
(with Sheila Walsh)

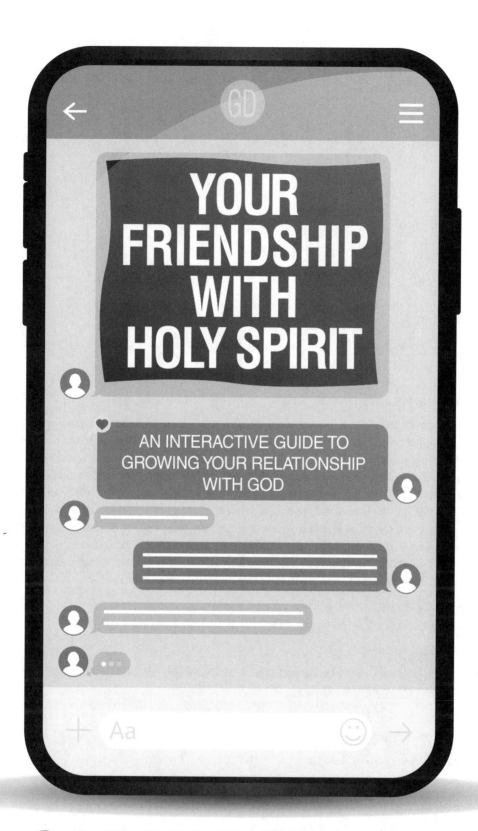

YOUR FRIENDSHIP WITH HOLY SPIRIT

AN INTERACTIVE GUIDE TO GROWING YOUR RELATIONSHIP WITH GOD

SARAH BOWLING

DESTINY IMAGE® PUBLISHERS, INC.

P.O. Box 310, Shippensburg, PA 17257-0310

"Promoting Inspired Lives."

This book and all other Destiny Image and Destiny Image Fiction books are available at Christian bookstores and distributors worldwide.

For more information on foreign distributors, call 717-532-3040.

Reach us on the Internet: www.destinyimage.com.

ISBN 13 TP: 978-0-7684-5931-9

ISBN 13 eBook: 978-0-7684-5932-6

For Worldwide Distribution, Printed in the U.S.A.

1 2 3 4 5 6 7 8 / 25 24 23 22 21

DEDICATION

I dedicate this book to anyone who struggles with relationships. I pray that your journey to grow closer with Holy Spirit will also help your relationships with humans. May Holy Spirit be your Helper in all relational contexts!

ACKNOWLEDGMENTS

I thank Sarah Heaton who read my initial thoughts for this guide and encouraged me to "Go big!" Thank you, Sarah, for being so encouraging and compelling me to make this guide available to everyone and not only a "qualified minority."

I also thank Encounter Church, my spiritual family, for being supportive and connected with me in this journey. Thank you more than I can express for being community!

Finally and most importantly, I thank Holy Spirit for being my relationship anchor, life jacket, sun on the horizon, EMT, steady friend, wise counsel, parent of all parents, and continual companion. I'm alive because of Your genuine love!

CONTENTS

Foreword 11

Introduction 13

Chapter 1   Nice to Meet You! 15

Chapter 2   Who Are You? 29

Chapter 3   What Are Some Obstacles? 39

Chapter 4   Truth or Trick? 49

Chapter 5   Who's Your Momma? 63

Chapter 6   Do the Student Thing 77

Chapter 7   Be a Raving Fan! 91

Chapter 8   Do You Want an Upgrade? 103

Chapter 9   Being Expressive 119

Chapter 10   The No-Go Zone 135

Chapter 11   Let's Go! 147

About the Author 159

FOREWORD

Living and loving like Jesus in a broken world should be the desire of every disciple of Christ. One of the most radical revelations is that Christ lives within you. The Spirit of God who raised Jesus from the dead lives in you!

If the Holy Spirit dwells in and with me, His Spirit has made His home in my spirit. The Son of God is on the inside. He has clothed Himself with my flesh. What would the world look like if the average believer lived in this way—His presence in us, not just filling a space but in us?

The Holy Spirit is God and is a person. My wife is a person with a name, Jennifer; she is my friend, companion, lover, advisor, comforter, and mother to our children. After 32 years of sharing life together, we know each other very well.

The Holy Spirit is also a person, friend, life coach, counselor, and God. The Spirit lives in me and for the last 36 years, the Spirit has given me strength, power, joy, wisdom, peace and freedom. In the last year I have had a deep desire to build a more meaningful relationship with Holy Spirit. My prayer has been: "Jesus, step into me and live through me as fully as You want to. Let me truly be Your hands, feet, eyes and mouth. Holy Spirit, let the world experience a God like Jesus through my life, Amen."

In my journey of longing for more, God connected me to Sarah and Reece Bowling. For the last three years, I have observed their intimate friendship and relationship with Holy Spirit.

On my last trip to Denver, I experienced a desire to befriend the Holy Spirit in a more meaningful way. After a day with Sarah and her mom Marilyn, my heart burned for more. Sarah shared that she was writing a relationship guide for connecting with Holy Spirit and she felt in the Spirit to ask me to do the foreword. It was easy for me to say yes because I knew Holy Spirit was her dearest friend!

The first time I read through the guide, I was overwhelmed by the presence and person of Holy Spirit. The second time, I allowed the guide to read me! So far, I have repented for times when I valued Holy Spirit for what the Spirit would do rather than valuing the relationship itself. It has refreshed my spiritual passion, personal revival, and given me transformation that will lead to reformation.

Your Friendship with Holy Spirit is timely, practical, and God inspired. Jesus calls His bride to arise and shine in a world looking for Jesus—to those who are searching, to those who are hungry, to those who are eager to grow, and to those who are looking for more of Him!

Jesus said, *"I am come that they might have life, and that they might have it more abundantly"* (John 10:10 King James Version). Many believers have a portion of this verse but not all of it. *Your Friendship with Holy Spirit* will help you in the rest!

—Leif Hetland
President and Founder Global Mission Awareness
Author, *Called to Reign* and *Healing the Orphan Spirit*

Introduction

I'm so very happy you have this resource in your hand, regardless of how you came to this moment. And I'm quite excited for you to begin what could be the best adventure of your entire life! I can make that statement with confidence because of my own journey with Holy Spirit that has included lots of surprises, discoveries, blind curves, gifts, lessons, and heaps more.

This book is written as a relationship guide, so it's intended to be more interactive than informational. If you're keen to have more information about Holy Spirit, please grab my books *Heavenly Help* and *In Step With the Spirit*. They will give you some helpful content and insightful applications.

This interactive relationship guide includes building blocks for cultivating an ever-deepening connection with Holy Spirit. Each chapter has several interactive components, such as assessments, activities, connection exercises, and more. At the end of each chapter, you'll also find discussion questions that could be helpful for either small group conversations or individual exploration.

If you approach this resource *solely* as a study guide for acquiring information, or if you are endeavoring to use Holy Spirit for more power or to gain supernatural demonstrations in your life, there is a good chance this guide will not meet your expectations. To be sure, more information, power, and demonstration could definitely be by-products of cultivating a greater connection and intimacy with Holy Spirit. But let's keep the main thing—connection with Holy Spirit—the main thing, with lots of freedom and flexibility for expression, consequences, demonstrations, supernatural evidence, and character growth as possible results of deepening intimacy with Holy Spirit.

I want to encourage you strongly to keep an open mind as you process and journey through this relationship guide. I recognize that individuals from diverse backgrounds will be going through this book, which means that people who have no experience or education with Holy Spirit will be using this guide right alongside people who consider themselves well-versed in all things Holy Spirit. No matter your background, please don't limit the possibility of deepening your connection with Holy Spirit with preconceived ideas that either disqualify or over-qualify you through ignorance or expertise.

As our road map for growing our connection with Holy Spirit, we will be using Jesus' introduction to Holy Spirit found in the book of John chapters 14 through 16. I prefer to start in these chapters, rather than starting in Acts 2 with Holy Spirit's demonstration on Pentecost, because I am firmly convinced that Jesus' education and guidance for Holy Spirit in John was the groundwork for the supernatural outpouring that followed in Acts 2.

Indeed, Jesus gave His disciples a Holy Spirit tutorial during His Last Supper, which was essential for their journey through His crucifixion, resurrection, ascension, and the dramatic display in Jerusalem more than fifty days later.

Consequently, if Jesus chose to give His disciples a Holy Spirit tutorial, then, as Jesus' modern-day followers, we would be wise to follow His lead and enjoy His training and guidance. Let's begin our wonderful adventure now and cultivate a growing connection with Holy Spirit!

Chapter 1

NICE TO MEET YOU!

The goal of this resource is to grow and deepen your relationship with Holy Spirit. To that end, a relationship can only be as deep or as intimate as each person knows themselves and the other person. Additionally, it's very helpful to know what you think about someone or what your perspective is so that you can be aware of any potential hurdles that might need to be overcome in order to get closer to the person.

For example, I developed an unexpected friendship in college with one of my fellow RAs (resident advisors). It was a delightfully surprising and wonderful friendship. It was unexpected because our interests were so different. Julie really enjoyed experimenting with makeup and hairstyles and getting manicures and facials—I didn't. To help the friendship grow and deepen, I had to come to terms with my biases and stereotypes regarding people who enjoy beauty products. Those biases could have become hindrances to becoming close friends.

Indeed, some of our stereotypes and assumptions often prevent us from getting close to certain people. I would suggest that this might also be the case for you when you start to build a deeper relationship with Holy Spirit. In order to cultivate a deeper connection, let's take some initial steps to assess our current awareness of and relationship with Holy Spirit. In this assessment, we will look at what you might know about Holy Spirit. We'll also look at what might be some hindrances you could have for developing a closer relationship with Holy Spirit.

The following are two essential first steps in cultivating any relationship:

- Who am I and what are my filters and predispositions?
- Who are you and what do I know about you?

WHAT ABOUT YOU?

Think back over the friendships you have developed over your lifetime. In the space provided below, list the people you consider to be your closest friends. Some of these people might have been close to you for just a season of your life. Some may have been people you enjoyed because you shared a common goal or activity.

_____

_____

_____

_____

_____

_____

From the list of people you made, identify at least one thing about each person that helped you to be friends.

_____

_____

_____

_____

_____

_____

From this same list of people, who do you keep in touch with somewhat consistently?

_____

_____

_____

_____

_____

_____

Who don't you keep in touch with and why?

_____

_____

_____

_____

_____

_____

I think it is helpful to consider the people who have been close friends over the course of our lives, because such recollections can help us identify things that are important to us when we connect with others. As we begin to talk about cultivating a connection with Holy Spirit, I want to bring these things to your attention.

When we think about our human friendships, it is easier to identify connections because of the tangible, visible, and audible nature of human interactions. In contrast, Holy Spirit isn't human. Connecting with someone who is invisible, inaudible, and intangible can be challenging. In this relationship guide, we are going to look at not only who Holy Spirit is, but we are also going to explore ideas about how to cultivate connections with Holy Spirit, appreciating your unique design.

I bring up your unique design because a relationship is made up of two unique individuals. Your individuality shapes and defines how you show up in relationships. For example, I have friends who are very high achievers. When we are completing a project together, there is lots of connection and conversation. When we aren't working on a project together, there is less conversation and connection. These friends are task oriented, and tasks are the medium for connection.

On the opposite spectrum, I have friends who are very athletic and activity oriented. Our interactions and connections center on exercises such as hiking, pickle ball, working out, snowboarding, skiing, etc. Other friends prefer to have face-to-face conversations and interactions. To them, activities or achievements can be distractions from deeply connected conversations.

And, of course, there are the friends who "pick up where we left off," such that extended gaps of time in between periods of connecting don't seem to be obstacles for remaining close.

Your preferred medium for connecting is an important consideration when thinking about cultivating a deep connection with Holy Spirit.

STEP 1: ASSESSMENT

Let's start with an introductory assessment to help you identify what you might know about Holy Spirit. We will also look at some possible assumptions or stereotypes about Holy Spirit that could be a barrier to cultivating a deeper connection with Holy Spirit. Additionally, this assessment might point out some things you do not know.

Who Is Holy Spirit and What's Your Outlook on Holy Spirit?

1. In what context is Holy Spirit first mentioned in the Bible?

   A. Jesus being baptized

   B. Pentecost

   C. Before creation when God's Spirit hovered over the earth

   D. Holy Spirit leading Jesus into the wilderness to be tempted

2. What is the primary or essential relationship group where Holy Spirit exists?

   A. With Peter on the Day of Pentecost

   B. In the Trinity with Father, Son, and Holy Spirit

   C. With Jesus when He's resurrected

   D. With Paul as he writes the epistles

3. What words come to your mind when you think of the word *Spirit*?

_____

_____

_____

_____

_____

_____

4. Circle all the things Holy Spirit does:

   A. Pours the Father's love into our hearts

   B. Convinces us that we are God's children (son or daughter)

   C. Leaves us to make us more independent

   D. Comforts and helps us

   E. Condemns our failures and weaknesses

   F. Floats in a cloud in detached observation

   G. Makes people act strangely and do weird stuff

   H. Zaps people with random power

   I. Remains an inert part of the Trinity

   J. Watches humanity with detached disinterest

   K. Makes us speak in weird languages

5. Have you had strange or unusual experiences with people who are Holy Spirit advocates? How have such experiences affected you negatively? Positively?

_____

_____

_____

_____

_____

_____

6. From the following list, circle all the names and/or identities of Holy Spirit:

   A. Spirit of Truth

   B. Comforter

   C. Accuser

   D. Spirit of Wisdom

   E. Advocate

   F. Helper

   G. Disinterested Bystander

   H. Resurrection

   I. Counselor

7. Describe an experience you have had with Holy Spirit that left a major impression on your life.

   _____

   _____

   _____

   _____

   _____

   _____

STEP 2: ASSESSMENT EVALUATION

Look at the following answer key and compare it to your answers. This exercise is for the sole purpose of raising your awareness of what your perceptions of Holy Spirit are. It can help you realize your basic awareness of who you believe Holy Spirit is.

Answer Key: Who Is Holy Spirit and What's Your Outlook on Holy Spirit?

1. Where is Holy Spirit first mentioned in the Bible and in what context?

    A. Jesus being baptized

    B. Pentecost

    C. Before Creation when God's Spirit hovered

    D. Holy Spirit leading Jesus into the wilderness to be tempted

    Answer: C - Genesis 1:2

2. What is the essential relationship group where Holy Spirit exists?

    A. With Peter on the Day of Pentecost

    B. In the Trinity with Father, Son, and Holy Spirit

    C. With Jesus when He's resurrected

    D. With Paul as he writes the epistles

    Answer: B

3. What words come to your mind when you think of the word *Spirit*?

_____

_____

_____

_____

_____

_____

4. Circle all the things Holy Spirit does:

    A. Pours the Father's love into our hearts

    B. Convinces us that we are God's children (son / daughter)

    C. Leaves us to make us more independent

    D. Comforts and helps us

    E. Condemns our failures and weaknesses

    F. Floats in a cloud in detached observation

    G. Makes people act strangely and do weird stuff

    H. Zaps people with random power

    I. Remains an inert part of the Trinity

    J. Watches humanity with detached disinterest

    K. Makes us speak in weird languages

Answers: A - Romans 5:5

B - Romans 8:16

D - John 14:16

5. Have you had strange or unusual experiences with people who are Holy Spirit advocates? How have such experiences affected you negatively? Positively?

_____

_____

_____

_____

_____

_____

6. From the list below, circle all the names / identities of Holy Spirit:

    A. Spirit of Truth

    B. Comforter

    C. Accuser

    D. Spirit of Wisdom

    E. Advocate

    F. Helper

    G. Disinterested Bystander

    H. Resurrection

    I. Counselor

Answer: A - John 14:17

B - John 14:16

D - Isaiah 11:2

E - John 14:16

F - John 14:16

H - Romans 8:11

I - Isaiah 11:2

7. Describe an experience you had with Holy Spirit that left a major impression on your life.

_____

_____

_____

_____

_____

_____

Who Is Holy Spirit and What Is Your Outlook on Holy Spirit?

It's important that you consider what assumptions you might have about who Holy Spirit is. Sometimes our assumptions can be significant hindrances for cultivating a deeper connection with Him. For example, you might think of Holy Spirit as a floating cloud who is disconnected from physical matter. Or you might think of Holy Spirit as God's power extension cord who is mostly useful for supernatural demonstrations. You could also think that Holy Spirit is for the kooky, hyper-spiritual people who need a heavy dose of reality. It's possible that you think Holy Spirit is the mystical expression in Christianity, not unlike other mystical experiences in various religious traditions.

Perhaps you're reading this guide with detached analysis, weighing your theological knowledge against what this guide expresses. Or maybe you're reading this guide for the simple reason that you want to know Holy Spirit better. Who we allow Holy Spirit to be to us is often influenced or defined by our opinions and outlook. So, let's be mindful of the opinions and stereotypes we might have so that we can be available for a deeper connection with Holy Spirit.

I would like to suggest that we finish this section with some awareness about Holy Spirit. Because Holy Spirit is the Third Person of the Trinity, I won't refer to Holy Spirit as "it." The word _it_ in the English language often refers to an inanimate object, which Holy Spirit is most certainly NOT! Additionally, I'd like to suggest that Holy Spirit could be referred to as either He or She since Spirit is gender neutral. I appreciate that, for many reasons, gender is a hot topic, but we won't explore those reasons in this study. Instead, we will refer to Holy Spirit as the gender neutral He/She, as Spirit, Helper or Counselor. We will endeavor to stay true to biblical terms and gender sensitivities.

STEP 3: HOW COULD YOU GROW?

As we finish this chapter, it's important for you to know and accept that Holy Spirit wants to have a deeper relationship with you than what you currently have, regardless of where that relationship presently is. If you're distant from and skeptical of Holy Spirit, then maybe a deeper relationship could mean less skepticism and a step closer. If you're well educated about Holy Spirit, maybe a deeper relationship could mean more vulnerability and giving Holy Spirit greater access to your heart and soul. If you already consider yourself very close with Holy Spirit, maybe a deeper relationship could be more real-time life engagement with Heavenly Help, receiving counsel and wisdom for decisions. It could mean greater awareness of Holy Spirit being with you continuously.

I would also encourage you, if you haven't already, to take a few moments to work through the "Who Are You?" questionnaire at the beginning of this chapter to help you recognize some of the ways you might prefer to connect with Holy Spirit. I believe this is really important, because you are unique. I am firmly convinced that Holy Spirit treasures your distinctions. So how you connect and do relationships is a vital ingredient for cultivating your unique connection and intimacy with Holy Spirit. This questionnaire can help you recognize your preferred ways of relating to Holy Spirit.

Journaling or Group Discussion Questions

1. What are some things about Holy Spirit that make you squeamish?

2. What aspects of Holy Spirit are the strangest to you?

3. If you're in a group, share some areas in which you would like to grow closer with Holy Spirit.

Chapter 2

WHO ARE YOU?

> "I will ask the Father, and He will give you another Helper, that He may be with you forever" (John 14:16).

"I can do it myself!" This has been one of my lifelong mantras, and I've taken much pride in being independent. As I have aged, however, I have come to accept that my insistence on being independent doesn't give me much opportunity to receive help. This blind spot has been an obstacle as I have tried to get closer to Holy Spirit. Remember, Jesus introduces His disciples to Holy Spirt as the Helper.

The Greek word for *help* that Jesus uses is *parakaleo*, and it literally means "to call alongside." This is a really interesting Greek word because of the variety of ways it is translated and used. In various English translations, *parakaleo* means "comfort, counsel, advocate, encourage, and help." The reason this word has so many different English meanings is because of its wide array of uses.

Initially, this was confusing and frustrating to me, because I wanted something more precise to make it easier to identify Holy Spirit. I asked with frustration, "Which description or translation is the right one?" In my heart, I heard Holy Spirit reply, *All of them, Sarah. I'm far more than just a singular definition or identity.*

So, I have chosen to use *Helper* as my go-to identifier for Holy Spirit, because it has the broadest application. It is also important to consider that *parakaleo* includes the ideas of mediation, legal advocate, therapist, counselor, encourager, comforter, and interceder. I have become increasingly appreciative of the fact that Holy Spirit can participate in my life in such a wide variety of applications and contexts!

Additionally, it is important to remember that Holy Spirit is part of the Trinity, based on Jesus' words, *"I will ask the Father, and He will give you another Helper"* (John 14:16). I bring this to your attention to point out that God is inherently relational. There are three of them and they all live in union with each other. Indeed, Jesus frequently talks about the relationships that exist within the Father, Son, and Holy Spirit (see Luke 1:35; 3:21-22; John 14:16; Matthew 28:19; 1 Peter 1:2). He reports that they are all cohesive but distinct.

Because the Triune God is relational and we are made in God's image, this confirms that we are made to be relational. I would suggest that one of our core and essential relationships in life is played out in how we connect with God. Since Jesus has given us Holy Spirit as our Helper, it is vital to our identity that we foster a growing and deepening relationship with Holy Spirit.

RELATIONSHIP QUIZ

Considering that God is inherently relational, I believe it is important to be aware of what your thoughts are about relationships in general. The following is a quick quiz to help explore your posture or outlook on relationships. Circle the letter that best reflects your answer to each question.

1. From a broad perspective, what relational **context** do you most enjoy?

   A. Texting occasionally to touch base or check in
   B. Exercising, shopping, cooking, scrapbooking, or doing projects with a friend
   C. Having long, in-depth conversations
   D. Going to lunch to pick up where you left off after long gaps in time

2. What do you most enjoy **talking** about with a friend?

   A. Sports teams, exchanging recipes, political happenings
   B. Less talking and more activity
   C. Experiences that have great meaning or have had an impact on you
   D. Catching up on kids and life events

3. How much do you value **help** from a friend?

   A. Not interested in asking for help
   B. I like help with some projects
   C. I like lots of help, because it affords lots of connecting
   D. I like some help, occasionally, but usually I prefer to hire someone to do projects with or for me

4. In terms of "keeping company," what is your **presence preference**?

   A. Less is more
   B. Occasionally, such as once a week or once a month
   C. Lots of time together, because time is connection
   D. Discrete block of time, maybe an hour, but not more than two hours

5. Identify and describe the closest relationship that you have had. What are the ingredients in this relationship that made it so close?

_____

_____

_____

_____

_____

_____

RELATIONSHIP ASSESSMENT

There are many contexts and preferences for relationships. Some individuals prefer more distant connections while others enjoy more interaction. Some individuals want very deep and meaningful relationships, while others enjoy relationships in more strict compartments or discrete interactions.

Add up how many As, Bs, Cs, and Ds you have from the quiz above, and consider which letters you answered more frequently. As you read the next paragraph, keep in mind your answers. These could help you understand yourself and the preferences that you have for relationship engagement and interaction.

In the quiz, the A answers reflect a person who prefers distant connections. The B answers apply to an individual who enjoys casual interactions that are often based around activities. The C answers reveal a person who likes very deep connections, and the D answers reflect a person who wants his or her relationships to be detached and flexible.

Let's be clear that I have created this assessment on my own, and I am not a psychologist or therapist. Nevertheless, I think having some understanding of how we prefer to engage in relationships is helpful. With such information, we can move forward toward developing our relationship with Holy Spirit. Being aware of our preferences will help us consider creating a greater openness to intimacy with Holy Spirit than what we prefer in our human relationships.

Having taken this quiz and looked at your answers, how do you see your relationship preference having an impact on how you connect with Holy Spirit?

Let's also look at the challenge of having a relationship with the Spirit who can seem misty, intangible, quiet, and non-human. Maybe the reason that Jesus introduces Holy Spirit as the Helper is because Holy Spirit seems to have so many non-human characteristics. Jesus wants to give us some handles and sticking points for connecting.

For this chapter's *Identify, Connect, and Deepening Exercises*, let's dive into who Holy Spirit is. We will use Jesus' *parakaleo* language, along with a few other descriptions for Holy Spirit.

IDENTIFY, CONNECT, AND DEEPEN

Identify

Parakaleo means:

- Advocate: the idea of speaking on behalf of or defending another
- Counselor: relates to having wisdom, being a counselor and/or therapist
- Comforter: some overtones of being nurturing, compassionate, and motherly
- Helper: broad term—*help* implies that Holy Spirit can be *helpful* anywhere in our lives

Circle the identities that feel most natural to you.

List the identities that feel awkward, strange, unclear, or foreign to you.

_____

_____

_____

_____

_____

_____

Connect

From the identities listed, pick one that feels that most natural to you. With that identity, pick a connecting exercise from the following list to integrate with that identity.

Activity connecting: Think about what your favorite activities are: walking, jogging, swimming, baking, cooking, playing/singing music, etc. Pair up your favorite activity with the Holy Spirit identity that you determined feels the most natural to you. For example, if you like taking walks, bring the Helper with you on that walk. Listen to Holy Spirit, letting the Helper direct your attention, observations, or conversations along the walk. Or if you like to bake, invite the Counselor to join your baking activity as you measure flour, mix ingredients, and prepare the dough or batter.

Communication connecting: Using the Holy Spirit identity that you selected as the "name" for the Person with whom you're connecting, start a conversation. You can have this conversation in a journal, as you're driving in the car, over a cup of tea or coffee, etc. You could also write a letter or email to Holy Spirit using the "name" that is most comfortable to you. After you've written the letter or email, create space for Holy Spirit to reply to you. Listen to what Holy Spirit might want to say, and consider writing down what you hear or what impressions you sense.

Where or when do you find your regular conversations to be the easiest or most enjoyable? Use that same place or time for conversing with Holy Spirit.

Time connecting: Using the Holy Spirit identity that you selected to be the easiest for you to accept, block some time in your week to sit and be present with Holy Spirit in that identity. This could be a quiet morning where you sit outside, or by a window with a view you enjoy as the day ends. Invite the Holy Spirit identity that you determined feels the most natural to you to join you, and take some time to be present with that identity.

Deepen

From the identities that feel awkward, foreign, or unclear to you, pick one of these to consider and explore. You might consider asking yourself some questions about this identity.

1. Why do I struggle with this identity?

_____

_____

_____

_____

_____

_____

2. List the obstacles, hindrances, arguments, and/or reservations you might have with this identity.

_____

_____

_____

_____

_____

3. Accept that this identity is a struggle for you, without shaming, defending, or justifying your struggle.

_____

_____

_____

_____

_____

JOURNALING OR GROUP DISCUSSION QUESTIONS

1. Briefly describe an area in your life where you're highly independent. If you're in a group, share the identified area of independence.

   _____

   _____

   _____

   _____

   _____

   _____

2. Briefly describe an area in your life in which you are highly _dependent._

   _____

   _____

   _____

   _____

   _____

   _____

3. Who is currently your closest friend?

   _____

   _____

   _____

   _____

   _____

   _____

4. Who is the friend you've had for the longest amount of time?

_____

_____

_____

_____

_____

_____

5. How do you handle conflicts with your closest friend?

_____

_____

_____

_____

_____

_____

Chapter 3

WHAT ARE SOME OBSTACLES?

Over the course of my life, I have had a massive variety of experiences with Holy Spirit. Some of these experiences were very powerful and formative. Some of my experiences were gentle and comforting. And yet other experiences were eye-opening and very educational.

I'll never forget the time when I was five years old and my babysitter failed to come pick me up at my bus stop. She had been confused about the time that she was supposed to meet me, and I was left to figure out what to do. Cell phones weren't around yet, so I couldn't call my parents.

As I started to try to find my way home, I was really scared; however, I sensed Holy Spirit gently walking by my side and encouraging me to keep walking. I received step-by-step impressions as to where I was to walk: down a sidewalk, up a hill, across a stream, and up to our house. When I arrived at my home, Holy Spirit reminded me about the hide-a-key I could use to unlock the back door. I let myself in the house and used the phone in the kitchen to call my parents to let them know I was safe at home.

In another experience with Holy Spirit, I was living in China for the summer and was startled awake from a violent nightmare. I remember trying to calm myself down by going to the bathroom and reading my Bible, but the images and residue emotions from the dream kept accosting me. Finally, I went out in the hallway of the dorm where I was staying and asked Holy Spirit to help me settle down and give me peace. Holy Spirit met me there. After about thirty minutes, I was able to return to my bed and fall back to sleep.

These two experiences communicate that Holy Spirit helps us in times of crisis, which is super comforting! But I also want to share that Holy Spirit can help us during a normal day as we live out our routine existence. During the COVID-19 pandemic, when we were all in lockdown and doing the work-from-home adventure, I endeavored to take a walk every day. It was abundantly helpful.

On these walks, Holy Spirit and I would talk about the stress of being locked in, the uncertainty of the future, various struggles from my childhood, present conflicts in relationships, and the weak spots in my emotions. One of the positive outcomes for me from the pandemic was the daily walk I had with Holy Spirit. I have also experienced many supernatural demonstrations and miracles because of Holy Spirit's presence. Some of these experiences include healings, supernatural information, divine direction, protection, miracles, and lots more.

It seems to me that we can have hindrances that prevent us from cultivating a growing relationship with Holy Spirit. For some people, supernatural stuff is problematic. For others, miracles and divine demonstrations are to be valued and pursued. These people gravitate to Holy Spirit gifts that are discussed in First Corinthians 12. On the other side, some people are very comfortable with Holy Spirit being character oriented and enjoy working on their integrity and the fruits of the Spirit that are discussed in Galatians 5, while the supernatural stuff makes them jittery. Furthermore, I've talked with lots of people who have asked Holy Spirit for supernatural help, such as healing or miracles, but they haven't seen or experienced what they requested. The subsequent disappointment can be perplexing and frustrating.

To be clear, all relationships have obstacles. I have often found, however, that working through those obstacles is a great way to deepen the connection we can have. The same is true for our ability to connect with Holy Spirit. In this chapter, we'll look at some hindrances and difficult experiences that might present challenges in our pursuit of deepening our relationship with Holy Spirit.

Let's assess and explore your own experiences with Holy Spirit. In the following assessment, circle all the letters in each question that apply to you.

ASSESSMENT

1. How much background do you have with Holy Spirit?

    A. None—Holy Spirit is entirely new to me

    B. Some exposure in religious contexts

    C. Interacting with Spirit-filled people

    D. Attend(ed) a Charismatic church

    E. Studying the gifts and/or fruit of Holy Spirit

    F. Believe that Pentecost was when Holy Spirit got promoted

2. What interactions describe your experiences with Holy Spirit?

    A. Hearing a priest or pastor talk about Holy Spirit in a prayer

    B. Conversations with other believers about Holy Spirit "extremists"

    C. Being prayed over to receive Holy Spirit by praying in tongues

    D. Experiencing one of Holy Spirit's gifts (healing, miracle, prophecy, etc.)

    E. Vague awareness of Holy Spirit from occasional mentions in church, prayers, creeds, etc.

    F. Hearing or reading an occasional sermon, podcast, blog about Holy Spirit

    G. Disappointment from not receiving a Holy Spirit gift

    H. Repelled by strange behavior a Spirit-filled Christian exhibited

    I. Speaking in tongues

    J. Supernatural experience that has influenced your awareness of Holy Spirit

3. What is interesting to you about Holy Spirit?

    A. Gifts of Holy Spirit

    B. Trinity relationships among Father, Son, and Holy Spirit

    C. Fruits of Holy Spirit

    D. Expression on Pentecost

    E. Demonstration in daily living

    F. Involvement in Jesus' ministry

    G. Descriptions and discussion in Paul's epistles

    H. Presence in daily living

    I. Presence in the Old Testament

4. What would you consider to be your greatest hurdle toward connecting more with Holy Spirit?

    A. Holy Spirit seems illogical, not well-explained in rational intellect

    B. Intangible nature: not seen, audibly heard, physically felt, etc.

    C. Bad experiences around Spirit-filled people

    D. Sketchy theology in sermons, podcasts, blogs, etc.

    E. Lack of personal experience with Holy Spirit

    F. Additional struggles:

_____

_____

_____

_____

_____

_____

5. In what way(s) would you be open to knowing and/or experiencing Holy Spirit?

   A. Power demonstration to include Holy Spirit gifts

   B. Comfort in your heart and soul

   C. Greater biblical awareness

   D. Character formation

   E. Help in daily living

What additional thoughts have come to your mind as you've worked through this assessment?

_____

_____

_____

_____

_____

_____

IDENTIFY, CONNECT, AND DEEPEN

Identify

In this section we look at some lesser known Bible verses that reveal and describe Holy Spirit's activity. As you read through these verses, underline the characteristics that stand out to you. Then circle the characteristics that you want to know better or experience more.

Isaiah 11:2 – *"The Spirit of the Lord will rest on Him, the spirit of wisdom and understanding, the spirit of counsel and strength, the spirit of knowledge and the fear of the Lord."*

Judges 14:6 – *"The Spirit of the Lord came upon him [Samson] mightily, so that he tore him as one tears a young goat though he had nothing in his hand...."*

Luke 3:22 – *"And the Holy Spirit descended upon Him in bodily form like a dove, and a voice came out of heaven, 'You are My beloved Son, in You I am well-pleased.'"*

Matthew 4:1 – *"Then Jesus was led up by the Spirit into the wilderness to be tempted by the devil."*

John 20:22 – *"And when He [Jesus] had said this, He breathed on them and said to them, 'Receive the Holy Spirit.'"*

Acts 2:4 – *"And they were all filled with the Holy Spirit and began to speak with other tongues, as the Spirit was giving them utterance."*

Romans 5:5 – *"...because the love of God has been poured out within our hearts through the Holy Spirit who was given to us."*

Romans 8:16 – *"The Spirit Himself testifies with our spirit that we are children of God."*

1 Corinthians 2:10 – *"For to us God revealed them through the Spirit; for the Spirit searches all things, even the depths of God."*

2 Corinthians 13:14 – *"The grace of the Lord Jesus Christ, and the love of God, and the fellowship of the Holy Spirit, be with you all."*

Ephesians 3:16 – *"That He would grant you, according to the riches of His glory, to be strengthened with power through His Spirit in the inner man."*

Connect

Something Creative: Do you have a medium for creativity that you enjoy? Is cooking a creative outlet for you? How about scrapbooking? Do you enjoy playing a musical instrument or singing? Or is painting or drawing something enjoyable to you? Perhaps you like to write, whether fiction, poetry, or nonfiction. Pick your preferred creative outlet and select one of the verses to express through your preferred medium for creativity. For cooking, maybe you could think about the ingredients from Holy Spirit that could go into the verse you've selected and identify processes to facilitate that verse—marinating, proofing, blending, seasoning, baking, etc.

Something Active: What are some activities you enjoy? These can be activities related to physical exercise—walking, weightlifting, jogging, swimming, team sports, yoga, etc.—or activities related to cleaning, organizing, decorating, yard work, gardening, etc. Whatever activity you prefer, select one of the verses and memorize it while you're doing that activity. As you memorize it, imagine how you could see that verse being active in your daily life.

Something Contemplative: Do you enjoy being in nature? Do you find it fulfilling to let a sunrise slowly brighten your soul? Are you a night owl who enjoys the stillness and quiet that happens when everyone is sleeping? Pick a verse from the list and find a word in that verse that particularly captures your attention, and then settle into that word. Let it echo in your thoughts, feelings, desires, and presence. Consider journaling or making a verbal memo about your experiences.

Deepen

As you review your answers from the Assessment in this chapter, bring whatever obstacle, challenge, hurdle, or struggle that you've identified as a hindrance for you with Holy Spirit in prayer. How do you sense Holy Spirit replying to this challenge? Are there some people you need to forgive? Might you need to repent for some unforgiveness, pride, independence, or something that could have caused some disconnect with Holy Spirit?

_____

_____

_____

_____

_____

_____

What step would Holy Spirit have you take to go a little deeper in your togetherness with Him? Remember that deepening doesn't always mean a twenty-foot dive. For you, deepening could mean a few inches in your pursuit of connecting with Holy Spirit.

_____

_____

_____

_____

_____

_____

JOURNALING OR GROUP DISCUSSION QUESTIONS

1. Share a hobby or activity that brings you joy. How often do you get do this? If you're in a group, take a minute to celebrate the variety of hobbies or activities represented by each individual.

2. What is an obstacle or experience with Holy Spirit that has been challenging for you?

3. How have you worked through hindrances in other relationships that are close to you?

_____

_____

_____

_____

_____

_____

Chapter 4

TRUTH OR TRICK?

Truth is a foundational ingredient in trust, intimacy, vulnerability, connecting, and communication.

Imagine a husband or wife's surprise when he or she learns that his or her spouse has been living a secret life that includes another wife/husband, different bank accounts, and a separate apartment. When the spouse thought that his or her mate was going on business trips and working late at the office, he or she now realizes that the other spouse was spending time in the alternate life with a second family. Upon this truth being revealed, the marriage disintegrates. This spousal deception and betrayal completely trashed any trust or intimacy they had shared.

A tragic story such as this one illustrates that any relationship that is deficient in truth will be on shaky ground. This accentuates the importance that we keep Holy Spirit our Spirit of Truth, as Jesus identifies in the book of John:

> **John 14:17 –** *"That is the Spirit of truth, whom the world cannot receive, because it does not see Him or know Him, but you know Him because He abides with you and will be in you."*

> **John 16:13 –** *"But when He, the Spirit of truth, comes, He will guide you into all the truth; for He will not speak on His own initiative, but whatever He hears, He will speak...."*

My book, *Heavenly Help,* talks about two forms of deception that are problematic: internal and external deception. The sad illustration at the beginning of this chapter is an example of external deception. This happens when something or someone on the outside deceives us. Such kinds of deception can include politicians, neighbors, relatives, advertising, friends, coworkers, and classmates.

The second form of deception is more lethal, in my opinion. Internal deception happens when we believe something that is false, misguided, inaccurate, or distorted. The reason I think this deception form is more deadly is because it is inside us, it is not as easily recognized as deception that happens outside or around us.

The following is an example of an internal deception that was very hurtful. I remember pursuing a friendship in my early 30s. I thought this person also wanted to be my friend. She was loads of fun, creative, witty, and smart, and she seemed to love Jesus. For some months this friendship grew, and I was super excited to have such a neat friend; however, I began to see inklings of uncertainty. There were missed appointments, curt phone calls, and long gaps between conversations. I didn't pay attention to these for a season, because I figured that good friendships are resilient. I believed that I could make this work with a little more effort on my part. After some time with these relational hurts becoming more frequent, I came to realize that this person was not truly my friend. She had used me as a friend of convenience until she had found the next person in whom she wanted to invest.

What she did was wrong, and I have forgiven her. But the bigger challenge I had to work through was my own self-deception. I had really wanted this friendship to work, to the point that I had overlooked external warning signs. I had also ignored some internal caution signs, and I had believed stuff that wasn't true. I had convinced myself that friendships are one-sided and that I was lucky to have such a cool person as my friend.

No matter whether we are deceived externally or internally, deception is bad, full stop. The good news, however, is that Holy Spirit is our truth vaccination for all deception. To this end, we can let the Spirit of Truth help lead, correct, and align us in both our interior life and our exterior life. Holy Spirit can help us navigate possible deceptions in the world around us.

In this chapter, we'll do a brief assessment and then move into the ICD section to explore ways that Holy Spirit can lead us into truth.

ASSESSMENT

Identify and describe a time when you experienced an *external deception*.

_____

_____

_____

_____

_____

_____

How did it make you feel when you found out about the deception?

_____

_____

_____

_____

_____

What were some results of that deception?

_____

_____

_____

_____

_____

_____

In relation to *internal deception*, this can be very challenging because it can be easy to deceive ourselves:

- To think we are something that we are not (an athlete, a scholar, a worship leader, a writer, a chef, etc.)

- To be oblivious to our internal biases and filters (things that shape and influence our perceptions)

- To hope for something strong enough that it distorts our sense of reality

- To live in worry, anxiety, or fear so much that we make decisions in response to that outlook

- To think that we are *not* something that we truly are (prideful, hard worker, intelligent, insensitive, etc.)

Describe an experience when your thinking was untrue.

_____

_____

_____

_____

_____

_____

How did you discover that your thinking was inaccurate?

_____

_____

_____

_____

_____

_____

After you learned that your perception was untrue, how did that discovery adjust your perception?

_____

_____

_____

_____

_____

_____

What could be some deceptions to which you are more vulnerable? Ask Holy Spirit to help you identify what might be some self-deception hotspots. These hotspots could be areas of pride, insecurities, fears, etc. From the following list, circle the ones you resonate with:

- Social interactions
- Athletic endeavors
- Academic efforts
- Creativity
- Clothing
- Weight perceptions
- Image
- Face-to-face conversations
- Solitude
- Self-control/discipline
- Adventures
- Family dynamics
- Travel
- Addictive patterns
- Large crowds
- Employment struggles
- Racial struggles
- Wealthy people

_____

_____

_____

_____

_____

_____

IDENTIFY, CONNECT, AND DEEPEN

Identify

Identify that Holy Spirit is the Spirit of Truth. Let's look at this on a personal level by answering the following questions. In this assessment, circle each answer that applies to you.

1. In what season or stage of your life have you been more susceptible to internal deception?

    A. During childhood
    B. Teen years
    C. Early twenties
    D. During adulthood
    E. Early marriage years
    F. Child-raising years
    G. During middle age
    H. During retirement years

2. In what areas or aspects of your life are you more vulnerable to internal deception?

    A. My skills and talents – I think I'm better than I am, or I think I'm less skilled than I really am.
    B. My physical health – I'm not as healthy as I think; I'm less athletic than I think; I try to do more than my body will allow because I think I'm stronger or more fit than I am.
    C. My relationships – with family, coworkers, friends, etc.
    D. My communication abilities – I think I express myself better or worse than I do; I listen better or worse than I think I do.
    E. My cognitive abilities – I think I'm better at certain topics than I am; I'm smarter in areas than I believe I am.

3. Which of the following have you experienced as a result of internal deception?

   A. Financial struggles

   B. Job challenges

   C. Relationship struggles with friendships, coworkers, fellow students

   D. Marriage hardships

   E. Addiction struggles

Summarize your answers, identifying areas and seasons in your life that are more vulnerable to deception.

_____

_____

_____

_____

_____

_____

Connect

1. In what areas are you willing to let Holy Spirit help you change your perceptions, appreciating that such changes will necessitate different behaviors?

   A. Finances

   B. Communication

   C. Relationships

   D. Physical health

   E. Time management

   F. Mental focus

   G. Family dynamics

2. List the main deception(s) that you're willing to let the Spirit of Truth change. Please don't say, "All of them." As great as that answer seems, it might be too aggressive too quickly. Instead, pick one or two to bring to Holy Spirit for truth calibration.

_____

_____

_____

_____

_____

_____

3. Take a few moments to pray and welcome Holy Spirit to work in the area(s) you listed.

_____

_____

_____

_____

_____

_____

4. How do you sense Holy Spirit responding to you from your prayer? What are some impressions, feelings, thoughts, direction, or feedback that you have? Please describe these in the space below. If you don't sense anything, come back to this exercise after a little time and list anything you have observed or sensed.

_____

_____

_____

_____

_____

_____

Deepen

What could be some aspects of your identity that Holy Spirit would want to talk with you about for greater truth alignment?

_____

_____

_____

_____

_____

_____

Would you say *yes* to Holy Spirit for this truth alignment? If you want to wait on this conversation, consider putting a reminder in your phone for a few weeks in the future so that you can remember to revisit this.

_____

_____

_____

_____

_____

_____

Would you consider sharing with a trusted friend your challenges of walking in truth with Holy Spirit?

_____

_____

_____

_____

_____

_____

JOURNALING OR GROUP DISCUSSION QUESTIONS

1. Share an experience when you learned that someone was deceiving you. What did you do? If you're in a group, be careful to be brief so that others have the opportunity to share on this topic.

_____

_____

_____

_____

_____

2. What would be a major area in your life in which you're vulnerable to self-deception? Are there circumstances or triggers that increase your vulnerability in this area? If so, what could be something that makes this vulnerability more difficult?

_____

_____

_____

_____

_____

3. Are you open or willing to let Holy Spirit work in your heart and soul on some weak spots? What weak spots would those be?

_____

_____

_____

_____

_____

_____

Chapter 5

WHO'S YOUR MOMMA?

Have you ever been abandoned? I'll never forget when my husband told me that our neighbors were moving. Our whole family was massively close with these neighbors. All of our kids were at each other's houses continually, our husbands went to weekly prayer meetings together, and the wife and I were continually borrowing pantry stuff from each other as opportunities to check in and regularly chat. Besides the daily friendship, we also took vacations and went on ski trips together. We shared meals and spent hours that were filled with boatloads of laughter and fun. Hearing the news that they were moving felt like abandonment.

I was stunned, and it was no easy experience to walk through with my family. There were many tears, much grieving and loss, and even resentment toward the new neighbors for a season. To varying degrees, I think we all felt abandoned. That is a horrible feeling.

I would propose, however, that being abandoned by a parent can be drastically worse than having a close neighbor move away. A parental abandoning experience can turn a child into an orphan, and the orphan mindset is fraught with feelings of insecurity, independence, isolation, rejection, abandonment, and the fallout of relationship and intimacy struggles.

To this end, it is noteworthy to consider that Jesus helped His disciples not to feel abandoned as He talked through His last days. He warned them for several weeks leading up to the Last Supper that He would be betrayed and handed over to be killed. But He also assured them that He would rise from the dead after three days. At the Last Supper, Jesus specifically stepped into the topic of abandonment and orphans. He calmed His disciples' fears and introduced to them how Holy Spirit would be stepping into their lives in His absence.

> *I will ask the Father, and He will give you another Helper, that He may be with you forever; that is the Spirit of truth, whom the world cannot receive, because it does not see Him or know Him, but you know Him because He abides with you and will be in you. I will not leave you as orphans; I will come to you* (**John 14:16-18**).

It is important to think about Jesus' words regarding abandonment and orphans to see the link with Holy Spirit in the preceding verses. We know that orphans have no parents, and they can often struggle with these issues. In addition, they can have difficulty navigating trust, self-reliance, vulnerability, and a host of other issues. Even if we are not technically orphans, we can wrestle with some of the same struggles. Our parents were humans, and whether they tried their best or whether we were neglected or abused, we live with the results of their parenting. Being aware of the feelings that we carry as a result of how we were reared is important. Jesus' words address the orphan or hurtful feelings that we wrestle with because of our upbringing.

For example, despite growing up with good parents, I have had to wrestle with abandonment experiences from my childhood. Such experiences included being forgotten at the bus stop when I was in kindergarten and being accidentally locked in a bathroom in Lebanon when I was five. While I grew up with good parents, I didn't appreciate how these experiences in my early childhood shaped my outlook and had an impact on my ability to connect with and trust people.

Upon reading Jesus' words in John 14:16-18, I began to think about Holy Spirit stepping into those places in my life where I unknowingly displayed an orphan mindset. Although my parents had never intended to abandon me, I still needed Holy Spirit's presence in those memories, and subsequent behavior, for healing and redemption.

It isn't a stretch to see that our heavenly Father can be the perfect Father who steps into our memories and resolves the shortfalls of our earthly father. I would also suggest that Holy Spirit can step into the shortfalls of our earthly mothers, to be a "divine Mom" of sorts. I understand that the idea of Holy Spirit being a divine Mom is somewhat novel, but I think this can be really helpful for people who have issues with their earthly mom. It is just like letting our heavenly Father help us resolve any issues we might have with our earthly fathers. Perhaps we would be wise to see our flawed, earthly parents as a dim and marred reflection of our connection into God's family.

This perspective can activate some very significant and powerful transformations in our lives when we intentionally allow Holy Spirit to step into the deficiencies that we may have from having grown up with imperfect human parents. Regardless of the strengths and weaknesses of our natural parents, it is essential that we recognize and embrace Holy Spirit being with us forever as our flawless Parent. We need to connect with our heavenly Father in the way that Paul wrote about: *"The Spirit Himself testifies with our spirit that we are children of God"* (Romans 8:16). Accepting and embracing that we are God's son or daughter is imperative. Helping us see and understand this truth is part of Holy Spirit's essential work.

Let's do some assessment now to consider how our upbringing with earthly parents, or a lack thereof, could have possibly affected our outlook, relationships, self-esteem, and more. As you go through this chapter, I strongly encourage you to open your heart fully to Holy Spirit to allow healing and the transformation of any wounds, scars, memories, or pain that you might have due to growing up with flawed, earthly parents. Remember that Holy Spirit is our Comforter, Counselor, Advocate, Spirit of Truth, and ever-present Heavenly Help!

ORPHAN ASSESSMENT

1. Were you raised by a mom and dad? If not, who were the main parental people in your childhood?

_____

_____

_____

_____

_____

_____

2. What was an abandonment experience in your childhood? Did your mom, dad, caregiver forget to pick you up from school, from a band rehearsal, or from a sports practice?

_____

_____

_____

_____

_____

_____

3. How did this experience make you feel?

_____

_____

_____

_____

_____

_____

4. What is a memory you recall from your childhood when you felt or experienced your parent or caregiver being very present, helpful, or engaged with you?

_____

_____

_____

_____

_____

_____

5. How did that experience make you feel?

_____

_____

_____

_____

_____

_____

6. Is there anything from your upbringing that causes you to struggle with relating to God in a parental way, either maternal or paternal?

_____

_____

_____

_____

_____

7. Where in your life today might you see evidence of abandonment or an orphan mindset? Consider places in your life—family relationships, work interactions, group projects for a school assignment, friendships, etc.—where you might exhibit extreme isolation, independence, rejection, detachment, difficulty trusting, vulnerability, etc.

_____

_____

_____

_____

_____

_____

8. Consider talking with Holy Spirit about these places in your life.

_____

_____

_____

_____

_____

_____

IDENTIFY, CONNECT, AND DEEPEN

Identify

From your answers in the Assessment part of this chapter, what hurdles do you anticipate encountering as you consider letting Holy Spirit be more parental in your life?

	No Problem		Medium Struggle		Massive Hurdle
Trust					
Money	1	2	3	4	5
Decision making	1	2	3	4	5
Time management	1	2	3	4	5
Total:					

	No Problem		Medium Struggle		Massive Hurdle
Relationships					
Friendships	1	2	3	4	5
Coworkers	1	2	3	4	5
Marriage	1	2	3	4	5
Family/Siblings	1	2	3	4	5
Attachment	1	2	3	4	5
Total:					

	No Problem		Medium Struggle		Massive Hurdle
Self-Esteem					
Self-image	1	2	3	4	5
Confidence	1	2	3	4	5
Narcissism	1	2	3	4	5
Shame	1	2	3	4	5
Total:					

From your answers, what area had the highest total, which reflects what needs the most attention? What area in your life is the least "needy"?

_____

_____

_____

_____

_____

_____

What of the following coping methods have you used?

- ❏ Achievement for value (performance)
- ❏ Medicating (drugs, alcohol, food, hoarding, etc.)
- ❏ Distraction (movies, gaming, exercise, reading, etc.)
- ❏ Relationships (codependence, isolating, shallow connections, etc.)
- ❏ Cutting or Self-destructive behaviors
- ❏ Other

From these identifying exercises, list the areas in your life that need help:

_____

_____

_____

_____

_____

_____

Connect

What can you do to let Holy Spirit step into the parenting deficiencies that you have navigated in your life? In order to connect with Holy Spirit in the areas where your parent(s) fell short, we must first forgive our parent(s) and/or caregivers for their shortfalls, violations, and weaknesses. Consider writing out words of forgiveness to your parent(s) and/or caregivers. If you aren't into writing, maybe take a walk and speak out loud your forgiveness toward your parent(s) and/or caregivers.

_____

_____

_____

_____

_____

When you forgive, it means you release the offending person from any acts of revenge, from your desire to punish them, or from your wish to teach them a lesson. At the same time, forgiveness doesn't include an open door for continued abuse, hurtful treatment or words, or neglect. If you would like a helpful resource to work through any forgiveness challenges you may have, consider reading or listening to *Total Forgiveness* by R.T. Kendall. He shares tremendous spiritual wisdom and practical applications.

From the list you created in the *Identify* section, take each item and fill in the following blanks with an individual answer:

Holy Spirit, I invite you to participate in this area of my life _____ to help me connect with You more fully.

Holy Spirit, I invite you to participate in this area of my life _____ to help me connect with You more fully.

Holy Spirit, I invite you to participate in this area of my life _____ to help me connect with You more fully.

Holy Spirit, I invite you to participate in this area of my life _____ to help me connect with You more fully.

Deepen

To move a step deeper and closer with Holy Spirit, how can we depend on these coping methods less and depend on Holy Spirit more? Check the box next to the activities you would ask for help with to deepen your connection with Holy Spirit:

- ❏ Take a walk, talk with Holy Spirit
- ❏ Tell a friend about a parent struggle
- ❏ Cut back on entertainment, amusement
- ❏ Join Weight Watchers
- ❏ Journal your thoughts, emotions
- ❏ Join a small group
- ❏ Memorize Romans 8:14 and 16
- ❏ Start a scrapbook for Holy Spirit as your parent
- ❏ Find a therapist, Christian counselor
- ❏ Participate in a retreat with a spiritual director
- ❏ Join AA
- ❏ Join Al-Anon

Action Plan: To deepen your connection and walk with Holy Spirit, list what you will do, create a timeline for doing it, and identify someone you will ask to help you stay accountable to this Action Plan.

_____

_____

_____

_____

_____

_____

JOURNALING OR GROUP DISCUSSION QUESTIONS

1. Briefly share an experience from your childhood when you felt abandoned.

_____

_____

_____

_____

_____

_____

2. From the following list, pick the most significant characteristic that is challenging for you and if in a group, share it: independence, attachment, isolation, trust, vulnerability, rejection.

_____

_____

_____

_____

_____

_____

3. If in a group, you might feel very safe to share your heart, or you might feel rather unsure about being vulnerable. Circle your level of comfort. There is no need to share this with the group.

Very Unsafe		Medium Safe		Totally Safe
1	2	3	4	5

You should sit with your answer over the next week and talk with Holy Spirit about your comfort level. Try to remain open to what Holy Spirit might be saying to you regarding this answer.

_____

_____

_____

_____

_____

_____

Chapter 6

DO THE STUDENT THING

When I went to university, the first major I declared was physics. I chuckle about that decision now, but as a freshman I was super keen on studying physics. I felt confident that I had the mental acumen to successfully navigate this degree. The first semester, however, was a rude awakening. I had significant struggles in my math and science classes and quickly switched to German, which I found pretty easy.

I had immensely enjoyed physics in high school, and I had received a fair amount of education in physics, math, and science. This begs the question: why did I struggle so significantly with physics in my university classes when I had so much exposure to it in high school? As I thought about this question, I realized that the defining distinctive was my high school science teacher, Mr. Brandhorst.

This man is a legend, full stop. It's quite possible that he was the best teacher I ever had, making all sciences not only accessible but enjoyable and engaging. I was neither super brilliant nor massively obtuse with science, but Mr. Brandhorst navigated me through vectors, Avagadro's number, moles, speed, centripetal force, acceleration, gravity, atomic weight, etc., with deft agility and clear instruction. Because of Mr. Brandhorst, I thought I could major in physics at my university.

Once I began my classes, however, I quickly discovered the power and significance of a master teacher—and the difficulties experienced with a lack thereof.

Changing my degree to German positioned me better for my natural abilities and released me from attempting to learn under people who weren't such great teachers.

Who is the best teacher or coach you ever had? What teacher or coach did you learn the most from in school, while on a team, or during lessons? What about this teacher or coach was so fantastic for you?

In the space below, list the things you appreciated about this teacher or coach.

_____

_____

_____

_____

_____

_____

Was this teacher or coach equally valued by your friends, teammates, or class-mates? Name some teammates or classmates who didn't appreciate this teacher or coach as much as you did, and why?

_____

_____

_____

_____

_____

_____

Teaching or coaching is a really unique talent and skill. For some, skillful teach-ing can be learned with the right attention, practice, and purposeful engage-ment. But without taking the effort to learn that skill, some people will never be teachers. I say this because of the two different outcomes I experienced as a result of having had two different snowboard instructors.

Cathy was fantastic. Her class had about six students and she watched each of us carefully to be able to give feedback, pointers, constructive input, suggestions, etc. She dialed into our individuality when she gave us feedback and endeavored to help us uniquely, and she did not expect us to conform to her teaching style or method.

In contrast, my second snowboard instructor was far less effective, because he wasn't a teacher. This instructor had two students, and his repeated advice to me was to "Get jiggy." When I asked him what it mean to "Get jiggy," he replied, "You know what I mean. Jiggy. Just get jiggy when you ride your board." This explanation didn't help me, and he wasn't able to come up with synonyms to help me understand what he was trying to communicate. Unfortunately, my lesson with him concluded with me being carried down the mountain on a medical ski patrol sled because I took a bad fall. My back was so severely injured that I couldn't stand up. Jiggy wasn't helpful, and this instructor was clearly not a teacher.

Jesus said, *"But the Helper, the Holy Spirit, whom the Father will send in My name, He will teach you all things, and bring to your remembrance all that I said to you"* (John 14:26). In this verse, Jesus lets us know that Holy Spirit will be our Teacher. The role of teacher is an additional way that Holy Spirit can participate in our lives.

Let's consider that Holy Spirit is the penultimate teacher who knows each student, recognizes how they learn, understands what is helpful and what is useless, teaches with words, activities, practices, demonstrations, modeling, and encouragement and gives lessons in bite-sized pieces so that students aren't overwhelmed by the learning experience. Holy Spirit is the Master Teacher— even better than Mr. Brandhorst or Cathy.

If we allow Holy Spirit be our Master Teacher, by implication this means that we are students. To this end, it is helpful to shift our perspective from the posture of being a know-it-all to one of remaining a learner. We want to stay continually teachable, pliable, eager, and ready to learn. Let's think about our experiences as a student and then consider what it looks like and means for Holy Spirit to be our Teacher.

What would Holy Spirit want to teach us?

ASSESSMENT

1. What are the characteristics of a teacher that you find the most helpful? Circle all that apply:

    Strong

    Patient

    Assertive

    Gentle

    Authoritative

    Attentive

    Steady

    Exciting

    Energetic

    Affirming

    Confident

    Knowledgeable

    Clear communicator

    Devoted

    Prepared

    Creative

    Flexible

    Listener

    Disciplined

    Organized

    Welcoming

2. What do you enjoy learning about the most? Circle all that apply:

History

Politics

Languages

Athletic skills

Relationship principles

Spiritual assistance

Practical skills

Cooking

Math

How things work

Creative outlets

New things

How the world works

3. Describe your best experience as a student. What components made this experience so great?

_____

_____

_____

_____

_____

_____

4. Describe your worst experience as a student. What components made this experience so awful?

_____

_____

_____

_____

_____

_____

5. Do you have some prejudices, mindsets, or obstacles toward learning that you think would make you a difficult student to teach?

_____

_____

_____

_____

_____

_____

6. Do you have any learning disabilities or impairments that might leave a sour impression in your mind about learning?

_____

_____

_____

_____

_____

_____

IDENTIFY, CONNECT, AND DEEPEN

Identify

1. List three areas in your life where you would like Holy Spirit to teach you, help you grow, develop, or change.

_____

_____

_____

_____

_____

_____

2. In what areas of your life do you think Holy Spirit would want to teach you?

_____

_____

_____

_____

_____

_____

Connect

What are some ways that you learn the best? Check all that apply:

Reading a book

Watching a YouTube video

Taking a lesson

Trying the activity

Listening to a tutorial, podcast

Imagining the activity

Real-time observation

Q&A

Lots of practice

Self-directed

Apprentice system

Quizzes, Tests

Constructive feedback

Affirmation

Tutoring, Coaching

Other _____

From the list, circle the words that describe your favorite, most effective ways to learn.

_____

_____

_____

_____

_____

_____

Write out the methods you circled in the space below.

_____

_____

_____

_____

_____

_____

Looking at those methods, how do you envision Holy Spirit teaching you?

_____

_____

_____

_____

_____

_____

Consider completing the following actions to give Holy Spirit the freedom and permission in your life to teach you:

Invite Holy Spirit to teach you, and then try to be aware of the times that the lessons are happening.

_____

_____

_____

_____

_____

How can you participate with Holy Spirit as you are being taught?

_____

_____

_____

_____

_____

_____

What input or feedback is Holy Spirit giving you during these lessons?

_____

_____

_____

_____

_____

_____

Coaching in Real Time

In what ways is Holy Spirit validating your learning experience?

_____

_____

_____

_____

_____

_____

What is your progress inventory? How are you growing and/or changing?

_____

_____

_____

_____

_____

_____

How could Holy Spirit be correcting, disciplining, or convicting you?

_____

_____

_____

_____

_____

_____

Deepen

In my book *Heavenly Help*, I give ten suggestions to help us be better students, learners. From these ten suggestions, circle a few that you would like Holy Spirit to help you with:

1. Focus on the right subjects
2. Pay attention
3. Bring problems to the Helper
4. Grow your trust
5. Respect the Helper
6. Keep at it, perseverance
7. Check your perspective
8. Be curious
9. Look deeper
10. Be flexible

One of the ways to go deeper in your relationship with Holy Spirit is to increase your awareness of Him. Jesus says that Holy Spirit is always with us, which lets us know that we don't need to ask for Holy Spirit to come. Instead, it can be a really powerful prayer to ask for greater awareness of Holy Spirit in our daily living.

JOURNALING OR GROUP DISCUSSION QUESTIONS

1. Share an experience in your life when you recognized that Holy Spirit was teaching you. What was this experience like? What were the outcomes of Holy Spirit teaching you in this experience?

_____

_____

_____

_____

_____

_____

2. Is it possible that Holy Spirit could be teaching you in ways or using methods that you are unaware of? What might some of these be? If you're in a small group, share your thoughts with the group.

_____

_____

_____

_____

_____

_____

3. Are there lessons Holy Spirit wants to teach you that you might be less than eager to learn? What could those lessons be?

_____

_____

_____

_____

_____

_____

Chapter 7

BE A RAVING FAN!

Have you ever heard of an AeroPress? This little contraption is the coolest coffee maker I've ever seen. I love it so much that I have one that permanently stays in my suitcase so that I don't forget it when I travel. My second AeroPress lives on my kitchen counter for easy access in the early mornings when I'm barely awake. If you're around me and the word *coffee* is mentioned, you can rest assured that I'm going to give you an earful about this coffee maker. There is also a good chance that you will receive an Amazon delivery within the next week that includes your very own AeroPress. I'm a raving fan of this coffee maker—an evangelist of sorts—and I am always ready with testimonies and examples of why this contraption is so fantastic.

I have shared this example about my love for the AeroPress to model what it could look like to be a raving fan for Jesus. The enthusiasm that I demonstrate, the commitment to the product that I have, the stories that I am eager to share, and the willingness to share my love for the AeroPress qualifies me as a raving fan—and all of these traits can be applied to our enthusiasm for Jesus. I like the term *raving fan* to replace the words *witness* or *testify,* because witness and testify aren't as commonly used; therefore, they are not as understood in the context of being a fan or promoter.

As we continue to cultivate our connection and relationship with Holy Spirit, it is helpful to appreciate that one important aspect of what Holy Spirit does is promote Jesus: *"When the Helper comes, whom I will send to you from the Father, that is the Spirit of truth who proceeds from the Father, He will testify*

YOUR FRIENDSHIP WITH HOLY SPIRIT

about Me, and you will testify also, because you have been with Me from the beginning" (John 15:26-27).

When I think about witnessing or testifying about Jesus, my mind can swirl around images of people wearing sandwich board signs or using megaphones to call their audience toward repentance—or sometimes to warn of the ending of the world. I also think about participants of various religions who go door to door endeavoring to share their faith and create converts. Witnessing or evangelizing can involve very strong and overt actions.

As I demonstrated with my zeal for the AeroPress, a person can be an evangelist or strong proponent of many things. Not all evangelists are limited to religion. Another example of me promoting something I'm passionate about is my interest in pickleball. Pickleball fever has become contagious in my world. I caught the pickleball bug from my friend, and I have infected many of my family and friends with it. In the same way, evangelizing or witnessing does not have to reflect the actions of a fanatic. The act of being a witness or proponent can be agreeable with our personalities and perspectives.

When we think about being a raving fan or a witness, we should consider two important ingredients for Holy Spirit helping us: personality and passion. Some personalities are naturally designed to be overt and aggressive, while others don't have the overt or direct groove. Neither personality is superior. Both are unique and essential. Regardless of our personalities, we all have things we are passionate about. Thinking about such passions can help us make connections in our pursuit of becoming a raving fan for Jesus.

It is helpful to think about what sparks your fire or what makes you excited. Some people are naturally passionate about witnessing and sharing about Jesus. Other people, however, find the idea of overt witnessing to be uncomfortable, awkward, intimidating, or even repugnant. If this is you, you might get nervous when Jesus talks about Holy Spirit witnessing about Jesus through us.

This is why I bring up the topic of identifying what you are passionate about. Our passions and interests can be comfortable and natural contexts for sharing what Jesus has done in our lives, for praying for others, and for expressing Jesus' life in our daily existence. These are all viable and authentic ways to promote Jesus that could be more comfortable and natural for you.

4

In the following Assessment, we explore your passions and personality to discover some ideas and possibilities for Holy Spirit promoting Jesus through you.

CAN I GET A WITNESS ASSESSMENT

1. How would you describe yourself? Circle all that apply.

Extrovert	Energetic
Introvert	Reserved
Analytical	Quiet
Compliant	Quirky
Rebel	Intelligent
Reflective	Simple
Impulsive	Steady
Friendly	Methodical
Cautious	Studious
Creative	Boisterous
Meticulous	Outspoken
Loyal	Sensitive
Adventurous	Detailed
Talkative	

2. List your hobbies, passions, and interests.

_____

_____

_____

_____

_____

_____

3. How do you talk about your passions, hobbies, or interests? With enthusiasm? With mild attention? Disinterest? Disdain or even silence?

_____

_____

_____

_____

_____

_____

4. What things are you a raving fan for?

_____

_____

_____

_____

_____

_____

5. On a scale of 1 to 5, with 5 being agreeable and 1 being repulsive, look at the list and mark your level of comfort associated with each activity:

Praying for someone at a sports competition:

1	2	3	4	5

Inviting someone to a book club that includes Jesus content:

1	2	3	4	5

Inviting someone to church:

1	2	3	4	5

Talking about Jesus with someone over coffee:

1	2	3	4	5

Praying with someone who just expressed a need:

1	2	3	4	5

Emailing, texting an encouraging word to a friend or acquaintance:

1	2	3	4	5

Traveling, international or domestic, to assist with practical needs:

1	2	3	4	5

Traveling, international or domestic, to explicitly share about Jesus:

1	2	3	4	5

Sitting with someone to keep the person company during a medical procedure:

1	2	3	4	5

IDENTIFY, CONNECT, AND DEEPEN

Identify

Describe an experience where someone talked with you about Jesus and his or her words were encouraging or appealing.

_____

_____

_____

_____

_____

_____

Describe an experience where someone talked with you about Jesus and it was unappealing—maybe even revolting to you.

_____

_____

_____

_____

_____

_____

Describe a time when you felt comfortable talking about Jesus.

To whom were you talking? _____

What was the context, setting?

_____

_____

_____

_____

_____

_____

How did the conversation turn out?

_____

_____

_____

_____

_____

_____

Why did you feel comfortable?

_____

_____

_____

_____

_____

_____

Describe a time when you felt very uncomfortable talking about Jesus.

To whom were you talking? _____

What was the context, setting?

_____

_____

_____

_____

_____

_____

How did the conversation turn out?

_____

_____

_____

_____

_____

_____

Why did you feel uncomfortable?

_____

_____

_____

_____

_____

_____

What could be your reservations for letting Holy Spirit share about Jesus through you?

_____

_____

_____

_____

_____

_____

Connect

How can you connect with Holy Spirit as it relates to sharing about Jesus?

_____

_____

_____

_____

_____

_____

From the reservations you listed in the Identify section, ask Holy Spirit to help you work individually through each obstacle.

_____

_____

_____

_____

_____

_____

List the activities you enjoy that might be comfortable contexts in which you could share about Jesus.

_____
_____
_____
_____
_____
_____

Deepen

On a scale of 1 to 5, 5 being total trust and 1 being total distrust, write the number that represents your current struggle to trust Holy Spirit to share about Jesus through you.

_____
_____
_____
_____
_____
_____

Consider asking Holy Spirit to grow and deepen your trust in the Helper. Write out a prayer that reflects that desire in the space below.

_____

_____

_____

_____

_____

_____

If you've had negative experiences from sharing about Jesus, bring each one to Holy Spirit and ask for help working through them.

_____

_____

_____

_____

_____

_____

JOURNALING OR DISCUSSION QUESTIONS

1. Share an experience you may have had when you talked about Jesus and it felt very natural and comfortable to you.

2. Share something that makes you uncomfortable about sharing Jesus, and take some time to pray for each other.

3. Share something about Jesus that is really wonderful to you.

Chapter 8

DO YOU WANT AN UPGRADE?

I heard my name over the loudspeaker at an airport gate before getting on an international flight. "Mrs. Bowling, please come to the gate counter to check in with the gate agent." At first, I thought that something was wrong or that someone had turned in something I'd lost. These thoughts ran through my mind quickly as I tried to figure out why they were calling my name.

When I arrived at the counter, the agent said, "May I please see your passport and boarding pass?" I quickly put these items on the counter. The gate agent did some work on her computer and then reached down to retrieve a newly printed boarding pass. "You've been upgraded, if you'd like to change your seat."

I was more than overjoyed. The international flight I was about to board was a long one, and any seat improvement would have been massively helpful. The upgrade meant I could sleep better in a more comfortable seat and eat food that was more appealing. Those perks would have a great effect on my ability to step off the plane refreshed and ready for my busy schedule. Of course, I'm more than willing to fly coach, because it is my normal class of travel, but I'm always very grateful for an upgrade!

I think we all like upgrades, and we appreciate them in lots of contexts: home improvements, car enhancements, phone contracts, computer benefits, etc. The word *upgrade* is a relatively new word that originates from the nineteenth century and means "to increase to a higher grade or rank." It is interesting that Jesus tells His disciples that Holy Spirit will be an upgrade for them when He goes away: *"...It is to your advantage* [upgrade] *that I go away; for if I do not go away, the Helper will not come to you; but if I go, I will send Him to you"* (John 16:7).

In this verse, Jesus talks about how the presence of Holy Spirit, in contrast to Jesus' physical presence, is an upgrade for us all. In full disclosure, I've struggled to see how this could be. When Jesus walked the earth, people could see, touch, hear, and experience Him as a human. All of our relationships are with other humans who are tangible, visible, able to be heard, etc. So how can Holy Spirit, who is invisible, intangible, and often inaudible be an upgrade or an advantage over Jesus' physical presence? I believe that it is true (because Jesus said that it is), but it is hard to understand. In *Heavenly Help*, I describe four ways that Holy Spirit is our Advantage: continual Companion, Confirmation, Guide, and Connection.

As our *continual Companion*, Holy Spirit is our upgrade from Jesus because Holy Spirit is always with us—*omnipresent*. You cannot go anywhere in the world where Holy Spirit is not present. Indeed, Holy Spirit is our constant Companion, even when we don't realize He is with us.

I have experienced the reality of Holy Spirit being my continual Companion in many circumstances, locations, times, and challenges in my life. For example, I'll never forget riding in an airplane from Luanda, Angola, to Frankfurt, Germany. On this flight, I became really light-headed and sick. I began to feel my face get flush and my hands get cold. I couldn't figure out why I was feeling so awful, and then I felt Holy Spirit remind me about what had happened throughout that day. I had endured a long road trip with almost no food. I felt directed to go to the galley on the plane and ask for some orange juice, which the flight attendant quickly provided when she saw how pale I was. I sat down briefly, drank two glasses of orange juice, and my blood sugar normalized—all thanks to Holy Spirit being my continual Companion.

Furthermore, Holy Spirit *confirms* the work of God in our lives, convincing or convicting us for improving our alignment with God's plans and purposes, as Jesus describes in John 16:8-11. I have seen Holy Spirit confirm God's work in my life numerous times, including confronting me about behavior changes, challenging me on various attitudes, encouraging me with open doors for ministry opportunities, and helping me sense Holy Spirit's prompting to give someone a Bible verse and encouragement.

Additionally, Holy Spirit is our *Guide*, as Jesus explains in John 16:13. To be more precise, Holy Spirit is our Truth Guide. When we follow Holy Spirit, we can be certain that the Helper will lead us away from deception and into truth. This is all the clearer when we consider that Jesus called Holy Spirit the Spirit of Truth (see John 14:17).

I have sensed Holy Spirit guiding me into truth on many different occasions. Some of these experiences include giving me wisdom about circumstances that my kids were going through, giving me insight into a situation that was confusing or unclear, helping me with direction for a decision that needed to be made, or sharing guidance within relationship struggles.

Finally, we see that Holy Spirit is our upgrade because of the *connection* Holy Spirit works in our lives based on Jesus' words in John 16:13-15:

> But when He, the Spirit of truth, comes, He will guide you into all the truth; for He will not speak on His own initiative, but whatever He hears, He will speak; and He will disclose to you what is to come. He will glorify Me, for He will take of Mine and will disclose it to you. All things that the Father has are Mine; therefore I said that He takes of Mine and will disclose it to you.

In these verses, Jesus says that Holy Spirit:

- Speaks what He/She hears
- Tells us what is to come
- Gives glory to Jesus
- Gives us what Jesus has

When we think about these advantages that Holy Spirit makes available to us, we can start to see how Holy Spirit can be our upgrade. I have shared personal experiences and observations of how Holy Spirit has been my upgrade so that you can see possibilities and ways that Holy Spirit could be your upgrade.

Take a few moments to do the following Assessment to pursue what this might look like for you.

UPGRADE ASSESSMENT

1. List the relationships you enjoy the most.

_____

_____

_____

_____

_____

_____

2. What is enjoyable to you in these relationships?

_____

_____

_____

_____

_____

_____

3. What friendships do you have that are not in close physical proximity?

_____

_____

_____

_____

_____

_____

4. How do you maintain the friendships that aren't physically close?

_____

_____

_____

_____

_____

_____

5. What activities or connections do you work on to keep these friendships?

_____

_____

_____

_____

_____

_____

6. How frequently do you connect or chat in these remote friendships?

_____

_____

_____

_____

_____

_____

7. In relationships that are close and connected, there has to be space and acceptance for the other's unique and distinct characteristics. To this end, what are your thoughts about having a relationship, connection with Holy Spirit who is intangible, inaudible, and invisible?

_____

_____

_____

_____

_____

_____

8. With the descriptions listed in the introduction of this chapter—continual Companion, Confirmation, Guide, and Connector—which description is the easiest for you to embrace? Why?

_____

_____

_____

_____

_____

_____

9. With the descriptions listed in this chapter—continual Companion, Confirmation, Guide, and Connector—which one is the most difficult for you to embrace? Why?

_____

_____

_____

_____

_____

_____

10. What is your biggest obstacle in seeing Holy Spirit as your upgrade?

_____

_____

_____

_____

_____

_____

IDENTIFY, CONNECT, AND DEEPEN

Identify

Describe a time or experience when you felt or recognized Holy Spirit:

Present with you

_____

_____

_____

_____

_____

_____

Confirming, convincing, or convicting you about something in your life

_____

_____

_____

_____

_____

_____

Leading you into truth

_____

_____

_____

_____

_____

_____

Connecting with you for greater awareness of God's work, things to come, and magnifying Jesus

_____

_____

_____

_____

_____

_____

Which of the following Holy Spirit *activities* do you want to have more consistently in your life? Circle as many as apply.

- ❏ Continual Companion
- ❏ Confirming, convincing God's designs and purposes in your heart
- ❏ Truth Guide
- ❏ Connecting with God for greater synergy, awareness of the future, magnifying Jesus

Which of the following Holy Spirit *activities* feels the most uncomfortable or awkward to you? Circle as many as apply.

- ❏ Continual Companion
- ❏ Confirming, convincing God's designs and purposes in your heart
- ❏ Truth Guide
- ❏ Connecting with God for greater synergy, awareness of the future, magnifying Jesus

Take some minutes to ask Holy Spirit to participate in your life more. Ask if there are any obstacles in you that would hinder Holy Spirit's participation. Write out in the space below whatever you sense or hear.

_____

_____

_____

_____

_____

_____

Connect

From the list of activities, circle what seems agreeable to you for connecting with Holy Spirit as your:

Continual Companion

- ❏ Physical Activities - walking, hiking, swimming, weightlifting, gardening, bike riding
- ❏ Creative Activities - cooking, sewing, painting, writing, decorating
- ❏ Achievement Activities - housecleaning, car maintenance, grading papers or tests, completing a business presentation, writing a paper, completing a project
- ❏ Reflection Activities - watching a sunrise or sunset, drinking coffee or tea on the porch, listening to a sermon or teaching, memorizing a Bible passage

Confirming, Convincing, Convicting

- ❏ Physical Activities - walking, hiking, swimming, weightlifting, gardening, bike riding
- ❏ Creative Activities - cooking, sewing, painting, writing, decorating
- ❏ Achievement Activities - housecleaning, car maintenance, grading papers or tests, completing a business presentation, writing a paper, completing a project
- ❏ Reflection Activities - watching a sunrise or sunset, drinking coffee or tea on the patio, listening to a sermon or teaching, memorizing a Bible passage

Truth Guide

- ❏ Physical Activities - walking, hiking, swimming, weightlifting, gardening, bike riding
- ❏ Creative Activities - cooking, sewing, painting, writing, decorating
- ❏ Achievement Activities - housecleaning, car maintenance, grading papers or tests, completing a business presentation, writing a paper, completing a project
- ❏ Reflection Activities - watching a sunrise or sunset, drinking coffee or tea on the porch, listening to a sermon or teaching, memorizing a Bible passage

Divine Connection

- ❏ Physical Activities - walking, hiking, swimming, weightlifting, gardening, bike riding
- ❏ Creative Activities - cooking, sewing, painting, writing, decorating
- ❏ Achievement Activities - housecleaning, car maintenance, grading papers or tests, completing a business presentation, writing a paper, completing a project
- ❏ Reflection Activities - watching a sunrise or sunset, drinking coffee or tea on the patio, listening to a sermon or teaching, memorizing a Bible passage

What necessary activities do you *not* like to do in which you could ask for Heavenly Help?

_____

_____

_____

_____

_____

_____

Deepen

From these upgrades, advantages with Holy Spirit, which feel the least natural or accessible to you?

Continual Companion, Confirmation/Conviction, Truth Guide, Divine Connection

Take some time to ask Holy Spirit to help you with the upgrade that is most difficult for you.

_____

_____

_____

_____

_____

_____

JOURNALING OR GROUP DISCUSSION QUESTIONS

1. What do you think about Holy Spirit being an upgrade in your life? Does this sound appealing to you? Perplexing? Curious? Uncertain? If you're in a group, share your thoughts.

_____

_____

_____

_____

_____

_____

2. How could Holy Spirit be more of a continual Companion for you in your daily living? What could be some practical ideas that you could use?

_____

_____

_____

_____

_____

_____

3. In what ways and contexts would you be open for Holy Spirit to confirm God's work in your life?

_____

_____

_____

_____

_____

_____

4. In what ways do you struggle to let Holy Spirit convict or convince you toward change and growth?

_____

_____

_____

_____

_____

_____

5. What areas in your life need more truth? Work, emotions, school, family dynamics, self-control, outlook, perceptions, money decisions, physical health, relationships?

_____

_____

_____

_____

_____

_____

6. In what ways would you like to have more divine connection throughout your daily living? If you're in a group, consider praying for each other to receive more divine connection in each other's daily living.

_____

_____

_____

_____

_____

_____

Chapter 9

BEING EXPRESSIVE

Do you have friendships you enjoy immensely, but there are some things about them that also really bug you? I have a friend whom I really enjoy. She's smart, insightful, funny, patient, and adventurous, and I like hanging out with her! There are some things that I don't like about her as well, such as her interest in snakes—a *major hard pass* for me—and in romance novels, and she can be too bubbly for me sometimes. I have taken into account the things I don't like about her and have still concluded that I want our friendship.

In the same way, this friend has also had to make her own evaluations and decisions about being my friend. She's expressed lots of things she likes about me, such as how I enjoy adventure, my enthusiasm for exploring various cuisines, and my love of quirky movies. When it comes to fashion and style, however, I can tell that she's not impressed with me. Plus, she has stopped asking me to get manicures with her and has replaced that with making witty observations about my nail-biting habit. Consequently, we've had conversations about our differences and have mutually concluded that we like our friendship enough to navigate the contrasts in our personalities. We see these differences as opportunities to celebrate diversity.

My decision to maintain a friendship even though I don't like everything about this person can help us think about some possible hang-ups we might have with Holy Spirit. Such hang-ups are important for us to consider if we are going to move forward with being closer, more connected, and more intimate with Holy Spirit. Intimacy requires acceptance, and such acceptance can include things we may not like or feel comfortable with. To this end, we are going to look at the results, or fruits, of being friends with Holy Spirit. In addition, we will look at the gifts Holy Spirit wants to give us.

We see in the book of Galatians, *"But the fruit of the Spirit is love, joy, peace, patience, kindness, goodness, faithfulness, gentleness, self-control..."* (5:22-23). I would suggest that these fruits are the result of being in fellowship with Holy Spirit. I liken this to what we experience when we have been around people and they begin to rub off on us, influencing our vocabulary or interests.

For example, the friend I referenced at the beginning of this chapter has had some wonderful influences on me that I've grown to appreciate. Being around her has caused me to be more friendly and optimistic. This is a direct rub off from her bubbly personality. She's also helped me to have a greater appreciation for clothing styles.

In a similar way, I believe that the more we are in fellowship with Holy Spirit, the more the fruits of Holy Spirit will be evident in our lives. These include even the fruits that might be challenging for us, such as patience or self-control. I've seen this play out in my life. As my connection with Holy Spirit has grown, I have been more aware of Holy Spirit's fruits being active in my life.

For example, I have seen some wonderful changes in myself related to becoming increasingly kind. I have not always been a kind person. I have a friend from middle school who shared with me, "Sarah, you were just flat out mean in school. You would tease people and it would often get mean, and even borderline cruel." In contrast, I now see the fingerprints of Holy Spirit on my life in the way I relate with others, having compassion in more of my outlook and being less critical. I attribute this change to having greater fellowship and deeper intimacy with Holy Spirit.

Additionally, Holy Spirit has gifts for us. We would be wise to look at these gifts and think about them being active in our lives.

> *For to one is given the word of wisdom through the Spirit, and to another the word of knowledge according to the same Spirit; to another faith by the same Spirit, and to another gifts of healing by the one Spirit, and to another the effecting of miracles, and to another prophecy, and to another the*

distinguishing of spirits, to another various kinds of tongues, and to another the interpretation of tongues (**1 Corinthians 12:8-10**).

These gifts are supernatural demonstrations of Holy Spirit's power, helping and challenging us to accept that Holy Spirit does what is humanly impossible. I've seen various demonstrations of these gifts that include people being healed of physical ailments, seeing impossible situations turn around, speaking in tongues, and lots more!

Two of these gifts—word of wisdom and word of knowledge—seem to be particularly accessible to me. I sense periodically Holy Spirit giving me verses and encouraging words to share with people that are very specific for their current situations. I have experienced these gifts on innumerable occasions. Words of wisdom and knowledge have come to me not only in church contexts, but also at a beauty salon, when I am grocery shopping, when I have been at my kids' school, as I have traveled in various countries, and when I have been on airplanes, just to name a few.

Saying yes to Holy Spirit's gifts and letting them flow through me can be scary, intimidating, exciting, unnerving, and even thrilling. I never claim to be perfect in letting these gifts flow through me—my humanity can make it difficult and I can make mistakes—but I know that as I practice, I get better.

For some people, these gifts are fantastic, exciting, highly desirable, and ardently pursued. For other people, these gifts are spooky, uncomfortable, unbelievable, and scary. But I bring them to your attention because both Holy Spirit gifts and fruits are integral to who Holy Spirit is. As such, if we're going to cultivate deeper connections and intimacy with Holy Spirit, it's important to be aware of these gifts and fruits, and it is important to consider our posture regarding these valuable components and displays of Holy Spirit.

Consequently, we are going to look at how our connection and friendship with Holy Spirit can have expressions and results in our lives that we might find desirable, a little unsettling, adventurous, and astounding.

GIFTS AND FRUITS ASSESSMENT

Gifts of Holy Spirit

Word of Wisdom, Word of Knowledge, Prophecy, Speaking in Tongues, Interpretation, Faith, Healing, Miracles, Discerning of Spirits

1. What experiences have you had with these gifts?

_____

_____

_____

_____

_____

_____

2. Which of these gifts are unclear or most unfamiliar to you?

_____

_____

_____

_____

_____

3. Which of these gifts seem more clear or understandable to you?

_____

_____

_____

_____

_____

_____

4. Which of these gifts would you most want to be active in your life?

_____

_____

_____

_____

_____

_____

5. Which of these gifts make you most uncomfortable?

_____

_____

_____

_____

_____

_____

Fruits of Holy Spirit

Love, Joy, Peace, Patience, Kindness, Goodness, Faithfulness, Gentleness, and Self-control

1. Of these fruits of Holy Spirit, which ones seem most natural for you?

_____

_____

_____

_____

_____

_____

2. Of these fruits of Holy Spirit, which ones are the most challenging for you?

_____

_____

_____

_____

_____

_____

3. Have you tried to cultivate and demonstrate these challenging fruits? How did your efforts turn out?

_____

_____

_____

_____

_____

OVERALL QUESTIONS

1. Do you have more interest in the gifts or in the fruits of Holy Spirit? Why is your selection more interesting to you?

_____

_____

_____

_____

_____

_____

2. Which seem to flow more naturally in your life: the gifts or fruits of Holy Spirit?

_____

_____

_____

_____

_____

IDENTIFY, CONNECT, AND DEEPEN

Identify

When you think about the gifts and fruits of Holy Spirit, which do you find more appealing and comfortable: the gifts or the fruits?

_____

_____

_____

_____

_____

_____

When you think about the gifts and fruits of Holy Spirit, which do you find more uncomfortable: the gifts or the fruits?

_____

_____

_____

_____

_____

_____

What gift of Holy Spirit would you most like to see demonstrated through you?

_____

_____

_____

_____

_____

_____

What fruit of Holy Spirit would you most like to see demonstrated through you?

_____

_____

_____

_____

_____

_____

Connect

Connecting with Holy Spirit around the gifts and fruits can be a wonderful adventure. With the *gift* that you selected, take some time to ask Holy Spirit to help you with that gift. This could go something like:

"Holy Spirit, I recognize that You have lots of gifts. In particular, I'd like to have Your gift of _____ flow through me. Would You please give me this gift? Thank You very much for being so generous with me."

After making this request, pause for a few minutes to be present with Holy Spirit and to receive this gift. Having paused, consider different ways and contexts this gift could be active in your life. List some of these ways and contexts.

_____

_____

_____

_____

_____

_____

With the *fruit* that you selected, in what areas of your life is that fruit *least evident*? Circle all that apply.

- ❏ Relationships
- ❏ Values
- ❏ Social media
- ❏ Conversations
- ❏ Work interactions
- ❏ Family dynamics
- ❏ Mental dialogue
- ❏ Money decisions
- ❏ Eating habits
- ❏ Exercise habits
- ❏ Time management

If fruit is a result of fellowship, how could you increase your fellowship with Holy Spirit in the areas you circled?

_____

_____

_____

_____

_____

_____

With the *fruit* that you selected, take some time to ask Holy Spirit to help you with that fruit. This could go something like:

"Holy Spirit, I recognize that fellowship with You can yield Your fruits in my life. In particular, I'd like to have the fruit of _____ more prevalent in my life. Would You please help me to grow closer to You for this fruit to be more natural in my life? Thank You very much for being so generous with me."

Deepen

To deepen your relationship with Holy Spirit, ask Holy Spirit to help you be more aware of when these gifts and fruits are present in your daily living.

For example, think back over the preceding day and look for Holy Spirit fruit being demonstrated in that day. Maybe you saw or experienced this fruit:

- Being patient in rush hour traffic
- Maintaining self-control in a heated conversation
- Experiencing genuine love for a coworker who is struggling
- Replying in a gentle tone to someone's snarky or sarcastic comment
- Choosing peace rather than fear or worry about a circumstance
- Being steady or faithful in a relationship when the other person isn't very consistent
- Bringing joy into a discouraging situation
- Doing something kind for someone knowing the favor will not be returned
- Choosing good actions or words by declining negativity or criticism

Consider that it is possible that more fellowship with Holy Spirit can facilitate more fruits from Holy Spirit in your daily living.

_____

_____

_____

_____

_____

_____

As for Holy Spirit's gifts, consider inviting more gifts to flow through your life.

_____

_____

_____

_____

_____

_____

JOURNALING OR GROUP DISCUSSION QUESTIONS

1. Share an example of one of Holy Spirit's fruits being expressed in your daily living.

    _____

    _____

    _____

    _____

    _____

    _____

2. When have you been the recipient of the fruits of Holy Spirit?

    _____

    _____

    _____

    _____

    _____

    _____

3. What fruit of Holy Spirit would you like to see displayed in your life more?

    _____

    _____

    _____

    _____

    _____

    _____

4. What gift of Holy Spirit feels most comfortable to you? If you're in a group, share with the group what gift this is and why it feels the most comfortable.

_____

_____

_____

_____

_____

_____

5. Pray Second Corinthians 13:14 for yourself, making it personal. If in a group, pray it over each person: *"The grace of the Lord Jesus Christ, and the love of God, and the fellowship of the Holy Spirit, be with you all."*

_____

_____

_____

_____

_____

_____

Chapter 10

THE NO-GO ZONE

As mentioned at the beginning of Chapter 2, "I can do it myself!" was my childhood mantra, and it still feels very comfortable to me now as an adult. In general, Americans esteem self-reliance and independence. The value that we place on independence can become an obstacle to welcoming Holy Spirit's participation and help in our lives. We also must consider that there might be other obstacles we could have when it comes to cultivating our connection with Holy Spirit.

The tenth chapter of my book *Heavenly Help* talks about different ways we might resist or ignore Holy Spirit. It's important to be aware of such mindsets and actions since they could hinder a growing and deepening relationship with Holy Spirit. The Bible is a good starting point to look at several different ways such resistance can happen. As we look at some of these verses, let's be open to the possibility that some of these things might apply to us.

For starters, there's a follower of Jesus we read about in Acts named Stephen. He was so passionate about following Jesus that the Jewish leaders saw his devotion as a threat to their authority. Consequently, they killed Stephen, stoning him to death and making him the first martyr for following Jesus. Just before Stephen died, he said, *"You men who are stiff-necked and uncircumcised in heart and ears are always **resisting** the Holy Spirit; you are doing just as your fathers did"* (Acts 7:51). What I find most disturbing from this passage is that Stephen is speaking out against the religious leaders who thought they were doing the right thing and who thought their piety and religious fervor postured them in proper relationship with God. These religious leaders were blind to their deception.

I make this observation because I think this deception also plays out in our modern existence. There are many well-intentioned religious leaders, as well as laity, who don't recognize their own resistance to Holy Spirit. I think this blind spot sabotages the transforming connection they could have with Holy Spirit.

A second way that we might resist Holy Spirit is discussed in First Thessalonians 5:19-20: *"Do not **quench** the Spirit; do not despise prophetic utterances."* This idea of quenching the Spirit expresses the concept of putting out a fire by pouring water on it. The word for *quench* in the Greek is *seenumi*, which means "Figuratively to dampen, hinder, repress, as in preventing the Holy Spirit from exerting His full influence."[1]

Paul continues his instruction in the next verse, specifying prophecy as one of the targets related to quenching Holy Spirit. I would also suggest that quenching, dampening, hindering, or repressing Holy Spirit is not limited to prophecy being restricted. We can quench Holy Spirit whenever we repress or dilute Holy Spirit's access to our lives, and whenever we limit Holy Spirit's demonstration through our lives. In the Assessment and ICD section of this chapter, we'll talk about how this might occur in our daily living.

Another way that we could resist Holy Spirit is through *grieving* Him: *"Do not **grieve** the Holy Spirit of God, by whom you were sealed for the day of redemption"* (Ephesians 4:30). This verse is sandwiched between two verses that discuss how we interact with people around us. The context for grieving Holy Spirit can be seen when we say things that are not edifying nor graceful to the people around us (see Ephesians 4:29). Additionally, we grieve Holy Spirit when we let bitterness, wrath, anger, clamor, or slander stay in our hearts (see Ephesians 4:31). It is sobering to consider that we can grieve Holy Spirit with the attitudes in our soul as well as the words we speak to others.

A fourth way that we could resist Holy Spirit is discussed in Hebrews 10:29: *"How much severer punishment do you think he will deserve who has trampled under foot the Son of God, and has regarded as unclean the blood of the covenant by which he was sanctified, and has **insulted** the Spirit of grace?"* The idea in this verse is that we insult Holy Spirit when we disregard Jesus and His sacrifice for our sins. The insulting of Holy Spirit is done by followers of Jesus, as opposed to nonbelievers.

The final way that we could resist Holy Spirit is the worst possible thing we could do. Jesus says, *"And everyone who speaks a word against the Son of Man, it will be forgiven him; but he who **blasphemes** against the Holy Spirit, it will not be forgiven him"* (Luke 12:10). The word *blaspheme* is a really heavy word, and it has the idea of aggressively attacking, treating with irreverence or slandering Holy Spirit. It's obvious from Jesus' words that we want to stay far away from blaspheming Holy Spirit.

In these five verses, we read several ways that we could resist Holy Spirit. Those ways are: quenching, insulting, resisting, grieving, and blaspheming. To have a clear understanding of each form of resistance, I suggest reviewing Chapter 10 in my book, *Heavenly Help*.

For some practical consideration, it's possible that we resist Holy Spirit when we:

- Refuse to ask for divine help in various situations
- Dismiss or minimize Holy Spirit's gifts
- Ignore the quiet suggestions we hear in our thoughts that are telling us to be patient
- Choose an unkind word instead of words of compassion or encouragement
- Scoff or secretly look down on someone who speaks in tongues
- Refuse to accept or explore a truth that is uncomfortable
- Don't welcome or allow space for Holy Spirit to do something supernatural
- Keep an arrogant or unteachable posture for spiritual gifts and/or fruits

As you read through this chapter and do the Assessment and ICD, let's keep an open heart to the possibilities of Holy Spirit showing us any areas where we might be resisting Him. Resisting Holy Spirit won't help us cultivate the life-giving connection He has for us!

RESISTING HELP

1. Do you easily accept help? List some examples of areas in which you easily receive help.

_____

_____

_____

_____

_____

_____

2. Do you struggle to ask for help? List some areas in which you find it difficult to ask for help.

_____

_____

_____

_____

_____

_____

3. As you think back over your life, can you identify seasons when you were more open to Holy Spirit participating in your life?

_____

_____

_____

_____

_____

_____

4. Can you think of seasons in your life when you were mostly closed to Holy Spirit participating in your life?

_____

_____

_____

_____

_____

_____

5. Can you think of times or experiences when you might have grieved or quenched Holy Spirit?

_____

_____

_____

_____

_____

_____

6. What do you think it means when Jesus talks about blaspheming Holy Spirit?

_____

_____

_____

_____

_____

_____

IDENTIFY, CONNECT, AND DEEPEN

Identify

In John chapters 14–16, Jesus discusses several characteristics of Holy Spirit. Such characteristics include:

Help	Witness
Comfort	Confirming, convincing
Truth	Guidance
Supernatural assistance	Continually present
Flawless Parent	Character development
Teacher	

From this list, circle the descriptions that are most natural or appealing to you.

From this list, write down the descriptions that are least natural or unappealing to you.

_____

_____

_____

_____

_____

_____

Is it possible that you have resisted, quenched, or grieved Holy Spirit in relation to the descriptions you identified that are less natural or unappealing to you?

_____

_____

_____

_____

_____

_____

If so, why are these characteristics a struggle for you?

_____

_____

_____

_____

_____

_____

Take some moments to talk with Holy Spirit about these struggles. Consider repenting and then asking Holy Spirit to help you with these characteristics.

_____

_____

_____

_____

_____

_____

_____

Connect

The places in our lives in which we have the most hesitation or resistance with Holy Spirit can hold the greatest potential for growth and connection.

Looking at the list of Holy Spirit characteristics that are least natural or appealing to you, consider doing some of the following connecting activities:

1. Select a characteristic that is a struggle for you and memorize two or three Bible verses that are related to that characteristic.

2. Select a Holy Spirit characteristic to talk about with a friend.

3. Consider doing a Bible study on a characteristic of Holy Spirit. Look up verses that pertain to that characteristic and look up what the root word for that characteristic is in the original Greek language.

4. Consider writing out that characteristic on a notecard to keep with you as a reminder as you exercise, cook, drive, ride.

5. When you first wake and as you go to sleep, think about a Holy Spirit characteristic. Either think through the day you just experienced with that characteristic in mind, or commit to looking for that characteristic to be present in your day to come.

_____

_____

_____

_____

_____

_____

Deepen

To deepen your relationship with Holy Spirit, pray for Holy Spirit to help you be more aware of His presence in your daily living, to increase your sensitivity, and to heighten your recognition of Holy Spirit. Ask Holy Spirit to make you aware of when you could be resisting, quenching, or grieving Him, and ask Holy Spirit to help you change your actions, words, decisions, attitudes, etc.

_____

_____

_____

_____

_____

JOURNALING OR GROUP DISCUSSION QUESTIONS

1. Share a time when you were resistant to Holy Spirit's participation in your life.

    _____

    _____

    _____

    _____

    _____

    _____

2. Share a time when you were welcoming to Holy Spirit's participation in your life.

    _____

    _____

    _____

    _____

    _____

    _____

3. Do you have an independent streak that might make connecting with Holy Spirit challenging? If you're in a group, share an experience that demonstrates your independence.

_____

_____

_____

_____

_____

_____

4. In what ways do you welcome and enjoy help?

_____

_____

_____

_____

_____

_____

5. When you hear the word *blaspheme* what comes to your mind?

_____

_____

_____

_____

_____

_____

NOTE

1. Spiros Zodhiates, *The Complete Word Study Dictionary: New Testament* (Chattanooga, TN: AMG, 2000), electronic edition.

Chapter 11

LET'S GO!

As we come to the final chapter in this Holy Spirit relationship guide, I'm excited to give you a massively helpful tool for continuing to cultivate a deepening connection with Holy Spirit. I started looking at and working with this tool several years ago, and it has been an incredible adventure for me that has overflowed with depth, maturation, connection, and relevance in my daily living.

My favorite discovery for cultivating connection with Holy Spirit is associated with the verbs related to Holy Spirit that are found in Romans 8. As I was reading this chapter, I did an inventory of how many times Holy Spirit is mentioned. I was astounded! I discovered that this chapter has the most references to and descriptions of Holy Spirit in the entire Bible—almost twenty mentions in approximately twenty verses. Within those mentions, I found nine key actions with Holy Spirit for our daily living. On a daily basis, using these verbs as a guide, I take each one and sit with Holy Spirit in that verb.

When I say that I "sit with Holy Spirit in a verb," I mean that I take each verb, in the order in which each are mentioned in Romans 8, and let Holy Spirit speak to me. I reflect on what He could do with that verb in my life. I pause and stay open to Holy Spirit's input, using each verb as a springboard for Holy Spirit connection.

I don't always receive solid input or concrete direction about a verb. Sometimes, what I sense is an impression, a tender nudge, or a soft feeling that goes with the verb I am attending to in that pause. The resulting connections can be powerful experiences, and they are often deeply settling and transformational. Such connections help lead me into ever-deepening intimacy with Holy Spirit. I want to introduce you to this adventure and give you some guidance as to what it could look like for you. I think you'll be astounded and encouraged to personalize and explore this adventure with Holy Spirit. Let's go!

We first look at each verb in the order listed in Romans 8. I believe that the sequence laid out in this chapter leads to a deepening journey and relationship with Holy Spirit. We'll look at each verb within the context of that particular verse in Romans 8 so that we stay true to the meaning within that verse. After listing the verb, we look at a brief definition of the verb and consider some ways that we could integrate that verb with Holy Spirit into our daily living.

Let's get started on this fantastic adventure!

Walk: *"...who do not walk according to the flesh but according to the Spirit"* (Romans 8:4). This word *walk* in Greek is *peripateo* and is a very commonly used word in Greek. It means "to walk alongside or to walk around." Each day when I start this adventure with Holy Spirit, I invite Him to walk alongside me throughout the day. I ask Holy Spirit to make me increasingly aware of His presence walking alongside me. In John 14, Jesus said Holy Spirit will never leave us, so it is very important to ask for increased awareness of Holy Spirit being with us. In this verb, I also ask Holy Spirit to direct my steps and guide my decisions. I keep my to-do list handy to write down helpful reminders for things I need to accomplish that day, because I often find that Holy Spirit gives me helpful reminders for the day when I pause with this verb.

Think: *"...but the mind set on the Spirit is life and peace"* (Romans 8:6). In Greek, the words *mind set* come from the word *phroneo,* which means "the perspective or outlook." These words point to our soul, which includes our thoughts, emotions, desires, perspectives, attention, and cognitive processes. In this part of the adventure with Holy Spirit, I invite Holy Spirit's help and input with everything pertaining to my soul. This verb prompts me to invite Him to engage with and direct my emotions, thoughts, focus, desires, and perspective. I very much need to have Holy Spirit participate throughout all of my soul.

Dwell: *"...if indeed the Spirit of God dwells in you..."* (Romans 8:9). This word *dwell* can also be translated into English as *live*. It is the Greek word *oikeo,* which means "to live, to take up residence, and to dwell." The emphasis on this word comes from the ideas of family, home, residence, and house. In my time with Holy Spirit sitting with this verb, I invite Him to live in me, to take up residence, and to make Himself at home throughout all of me. I invite Holy Spirit to rest in me, to be at home, and to be comfortable. I also consider what areas or topics I might be withholding from Him. I give Holy Spirit a backstage pass to my life and invite Him to dwell in all facets of my life—marriage, kids, community, work, travels, hobbies, friendships, values, decisions, etc.

Furthermore, the word *dwell* can be a very tender and intimate word, since home is where I relax, get comfortable, exhale, and just be. It is my intention that when I invite Holy Spirit to dwell in me, I am giving Him access to settle into the core of me and to make His residence in me.

Make alive*: "…will also give life to your mortal bodies through His Spirit who dwells in you"* (Romans 8:11). The Greek word *zoepoieo* is a fascinating verb because it refers to Jesus' resurrection. The verb literally means "to make alive," and it correlates with Holy Spirit making us alive.

When I first conversed with Holy Spirit about this verb, I was unsure about what to do. In my thinking, I was already alive and not dead. But when Holy Spirit and I talk about this verb, I often feel Him pointing me to places in my life that are lifeless, nonresponsive, or stagnant. When I follow Holy Spirit with this verb, I'm led to consider God's blueprint in my life. Am I living from and in accordance with God's blueprint? Is God's blueprint fully alive in me, or do I let my flesh or a distorted identity take up my daily living?

In this verb, Holy Spirit talks with me about who God has made me to be. Holy Spirit also points out the possibility that some of my divine design has been wounded or made comatose due to various circumstances in life, satan's efforts, human interactions, painful experiences, and trauma. In this part of my adventure with Holy Spirit, I bring these wounds and injuries to Him for healing, renovation, and regeneration. I want to fully live from God's blueprint breathed into my existence from the day I was conceived!

Put to death*: "…by the Spirit you are putting to death the deeds of the body…"* (Romans 8:13). This word in Greek is *thanatoo*. I don't like this word, because I don't like death and everything associated with death. Consequently, this verb is tricky for me; however, when I sit with Holy Spirit and this verb that means "to put to death," I pause and consider what needs to die in my life. This could include areas of deception, destructive patterns or routines, unforgiveness, distorted perspectives, unhealthy conversations, and deceptive identities that are not aligned with God's blueprint in my life.

Being led: *"...being led by the Spirit of God, these are sons of God"* (Romans 8:14). The word *led* in Greek is *ago,* meaning "to carry, lead, bring, or guide." The focal point in this verse is being a son or daughter of God. This is super important to consider because it speaks to our true identity. With this verb, I embrace that I am God's daughter. Because of this truth, I can be directed or led by Holy Spirit.

An important reason that this verb is so noteworthy is because we can follow after our earthly parents in our outlooks, our priorities, our relational patterns, and even in our destructive behaviors. Or we might run contrary to our earthly parents because of negative experiences or wounds that impede our connection with Holy Spirit. This verb, *ago*, is a critical necessity in our goal to align our identity as God's children and to be led by Holy Spirit from that alignment.

Testify: *"The Spirit Himself testifies with our spirit that we are children of God"* (Romans 8:16). This is a significant verb for us as we grow in our Holy Spirit adventure. It drills down to the core of our identity by divine purpose. This verb in Greek, *summartureo*, is the compound word *sum-martureo*. Here's the big deal: our true self is discovered and lived only with Holy Spirit's help and participation. The Greek word *summartureo* literally means "together witness or testify."

What is Holy Spirit giving testimony to in our lives? Holy Spirit testifies with our core self—our spirit or interior identity—that we are God's son or daughter. I welcome Holy Spirit to speak deeply to me, to convince me that I am not a spectator or an outsider in God's family. I am an integral part of this family. I invite you to sit with Holy Spirit in this verb, letting it become alive and resonate in your core identity!

Help: *"...Spirit also helps our weakness..."* (Romans 8:26). What would be some of your weaknesses, and what are areas in your life where you need help? You and I need help because we have weaknesses, and most likely these weaknesses are different from each other. Despite the differences, the reality stays the same—we need help. It is very meaningful to me that I can ask Holy Spirit for help. The word *help* in Greek is *sunantilambanomai*, and it is used only one other time in the New Testament. It is used in Luke 10:40 where Martha asks Jesus to make Mary, her sister, *help* her. So with this verb, I welcome Holy Spirit to help me in my weaknesses.

Such help includes not only my known weaknesses, but also the weaknesses of which I am unaware—the blind spots. The more I talk about getting help from Holy Spirit, the more comfortable I become being the recipient of Divine Help, to the point that I now delight in Holy Spirit helping me! As you sit with Holy Spirit with this verb, consider making a written inventory of your weaknesses. Doing this can motivate you to invite Holy Spirit to help specifically with each weakness. As you go through your list with Holy Spirit, pause occasionally to see what new weak spots He might add that could have escaped your awareness.

Intercede: *"...but the Spirit Himself intercedes for us..."* (Romans 8:26). I am amazed that He would intervene on my behalf! In the Greek language, this verb is *hyperentugxano*. It is only used in this verse in the New Testament, and it communicates the idea of Holy Spirit praying for us. This is a deep and powerful picture of Holy Spirit being in the middle of our struggles interceding for us. When I sit with Holy Spirit in this verb, I invite Him to stand in the middle of my difficult situations, challenges, conversations, struggles, and circumstances in which I am unsettled or inadequate.

As I finish this adventure with Holy Spirit, I am frequently encouraged and feel a deep and pervasive sense of peace and genuine love. It has been super helpful to converse with Holy Spirit through this journey on a daily basis, even though I don't always have the time to go through all of the verbs. There are many days when I only have enough time to get through the *dwelling* verb, or maybe up to the part about *putting to death* what is not aligned with my divine destiny.

Regardless of the time I have to spend on this exercise, and no matter how far I get through this sequence of Holy Spirit verbs, it is almost always a very meaningful experience. I encourage you to try on these Holy Spirit verbs in your daily living. Fasten your seatbelt for a magnificent adventure!

As a finishing observation, it is noteworthy to consider the tenses of the verbs we just discussed. In the Greek language, a present tense verb says that the action in that verb is continuous, ongoing, and doesn't stop. With this in mind, all of these verbs we discussed in Romans 8 are used in the present tense, with the exception of the verb *to make alive*, which is the future tense. This means that all of these verbs are for Holy Spirit action and participation in your life *now*. These verbs are not strictly for the past when Paul wrote the book of Romans. Furthermore, these verbs aren't for some distant future with no application for today. Every day, these verbs can be applied to connect you with Holy Spirit and to help you grow more intimate with God.

Here are some concluding suggestions to integrate these verbs into your daily routine:

Journaling: It could be helpful to take a page each day and write each verb alongside of what Holy Spirit is expressing to you. I have found that when journaling is done purposefully and with time and attention, it does not become mechanical or rote.

Work commute: Write out each verb on an index card, or put them in a note on your phone, and quietly speak them. You can invite Holy Spirit to converse with you about each verb.

Lunch break: It can be helpful to take some moments over your lunch break to think about these verbs and allow Holy Spirit to guide you.

Bedtime: Before going to bed, it could be helpful to purposefully consider each verb, giving pause to let Holy Spirit direct you.

As we finish this chapter, I encourage you to receive Holy Spirit's invitation to join this adventure for several months of daily discussion with these verbs. I think you will find your relationship with Holy Spirit will deepen, flourish, and maybe even explode! So, let's go on this great adventure!

In my journey with God, my central and continuous goal is to grow increasingly intimate with Him. I have learned that Holy Spirit is essential for this deepening intimacy. Jesus told us that Holy Spirit would always be with us: *"I will ask the Father, and He will give you another Helper, that He may be with you forever"* (John 14:16). Since Holy Spirit is always with us, it makes sense to get to know Him. Holy Spirit is part of our triune God and is paramount to our ability to grow in intimacy and connection with God.

JOURNALING OR GROUP DISCUSSION QUESTIONS

1. What are some ways you have come to know or be more aware of Holy Spirit from going through this relationship guide? If you're in a small group, share one of these ways.

_____

_____

_____

_____

_____

2. How do you feel about using the sequence of verbs from Romans 8 as a launching pad for connecting more deeply with Holy Spirit?

_____

_____

_____

_____

_____

YOUR FRIENDSHIP WITH HOLY SPIRIT

3. In what ways would you like to grow closer to Holy Spirit? If you're in a small group, consider praying for each other over these desires.

_____

_____

_____

_____

_____

_____

4. What might be some hindrances or hurdles you have for growing closer to Holy Spirit?

_____

_____

_____

_____

_____

_____

5. What is the main take-away or application you have from going through this relationship guide?

_____

_____

_____

_____

_____

_____

CONCLUDING THOUGHTS

It is my sincere prayer that going through this relationship guide has inspired and compelled you to cultivate a deeper connection with Holy Spirit, no matter where your starting point has been. As I've written this guide, it has become all the more obvious to me that Holy Spirit wants a deeper connection with you, regardless of your background, theological training, religious upbringing, deficiencies, frailties, failures, or achievements. I pray that this relationship guide lovingly nudges you to pursue a closer connection with Holy Spirit.

ADDITIONAL NOTES